FP

TIMMUR

STORIES AND FLAVOURS FROM NEPAL

PRASHANTA KHANAL

FP

Published by FinePrint Books
FinePrint Pvt. Ltd.
Bishalbasti Ka, Bishalnagar
Kathmandu, Nepal
Phone No.: +977-1-4443263, 4421641
E-mail: fineprintbooks@fineprint.com.np
www.fineprint.com.np

First published by FinePrint, February 2022

Photographs: Nabin Baral and Gagan Thapa
Layout and Illustrations: Ubahang Nembang

ISBN : 978-9937-746-49-6

Printed on Forest Stewardship Council certified paper with eco-friendly vegetable inks.

MIX
Paper
FSC FSC® C010615

Food is an epitome of culture. It embodies our history, tells our stories, and defines our identity. It connects us and divides us.

— Prashanta Khanal

Inside the Book

About the Book

CELEBRATING ETHNIC DIVERSITY

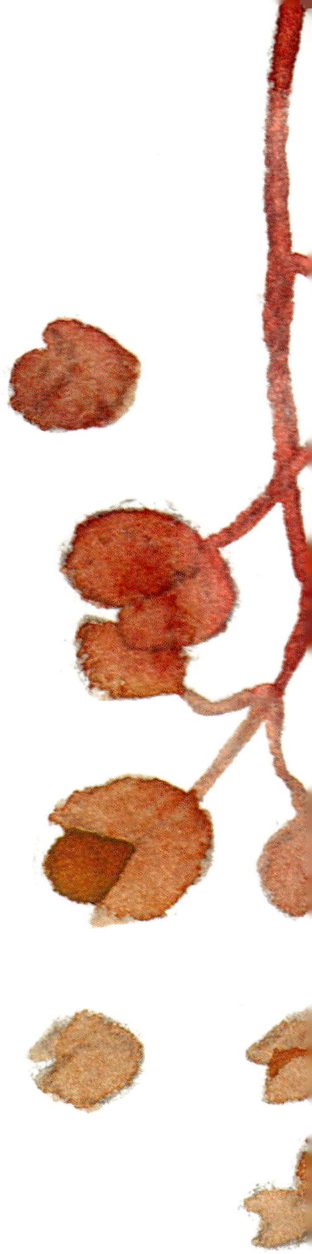

The quintessential Nepali flavouring ingredient *timmur* (Nepali pepper) can perhaps be seen as representative of the larger concerns of Nepali food and its connection to the land. Found wild in Nepal's mid-hills, this much-cherished ingredient has been used across the country for centuries, from the foothills to the mountains. *Timmur,* which comes from the same family as the Sichuan pepper, is peculiar and complex, combining peppery and citrusy flavours with the mouth-numbing zest of its northern cousin.

Like the depth and breadth of *timmur's* taste and use, Nepal's food culture is deeply complex and diverse. Its richness reflects the country's ethnic and cultural diversity, its varied topography, and its cross-border influences. Unfortunately, Nepali cuisine is often narrowly defined both outside the country and inside, failing to capture the unique culinary heritage of a myriad of ethnicities that call this country home.

This book attempts to introduce, celebrate, and promote the cuisines of various regions and cultures of Nepal. Many Nepali recipes, along with their ingredients, have a deep cultural significance rooted in specific socio-ecological surroundings. These traditions have long remained within the community, barely making the leap from their socio-cultural enclaves to the rest of the country. The hegemony of certain ethnicities is reflected in the standardisation of certain staples. Traditional recipes that were once an important aspect of Nepal's food heritage are now being forgotten.

Within these pages are stories and histories of more than a hundred recipes from across Nepal, including those the author grew up with. The book attempts to cover the length and breadth of Nepal: from the Sherpas and Tamangs of the Himalayan highlands, the Rais and Limbus of the eastern hills, the Magars and Gurungs of the Gandak region to the Khas-Pahadi community spread throughout the hills, the Newas settled within the Kathmandu Valley, the Thakalis of Mustang, and the Tharus and Maithils of the southern plains.

The various chapters in this book have been broadly divided according to the ethnic communities. Whenever multiple ethnic communities are presented within the same chapter, consideration has been given to ingredients, cooking techniques, and geographical, historical as well as cultural proximity. Such groupings should not be taken as an endorsement of a supposed homogeneity between or within ethnic groups. Rather, it reflects the inability to draw strict boundaries given the assimilation of these cultures and traditions. This book is by no means an attempt to parse all the layers and nuances inherent to Nepali cuisine, but rather an endeavour to provide a glimpse into the flavours that Nepal has to offer.

Hopefully, this book will not just be another Nepali cookbook, but will also serve as a repository for the symphony of Nepal's diverse food culture and its heritage. And finally, consider the recipes provided as a guide. Cooking, at its heart, is more about instinct, love, and the experience you gather along the way.

Writing this book was not a solitary exercise; it was only made possible with the help of many individuals, both friends and family, who kindly shared their stories and recipes and opened up their kitchens. This book is an ode to my mother, Dhan Kumari Shrestha, who first taught me to cook and respect ingredients. My parents and siblings have all supported me in one way or another in order to make this happen. I am very grateful to FinePrint and Ajit Baral for heartily accepting the proposal to publish this book. My appreciation also goes out to Shashwat Acharya, Priyankar Chand, and Pranaya SJB Rana for their help in editing, Ubahang Nembang for the design, and Nabin Baral and Gagan Thapa for the photos.

Nepali Cuisines

INTRODUCTION TO ITS DIVERSITY, HISTORY, & INGENUITY

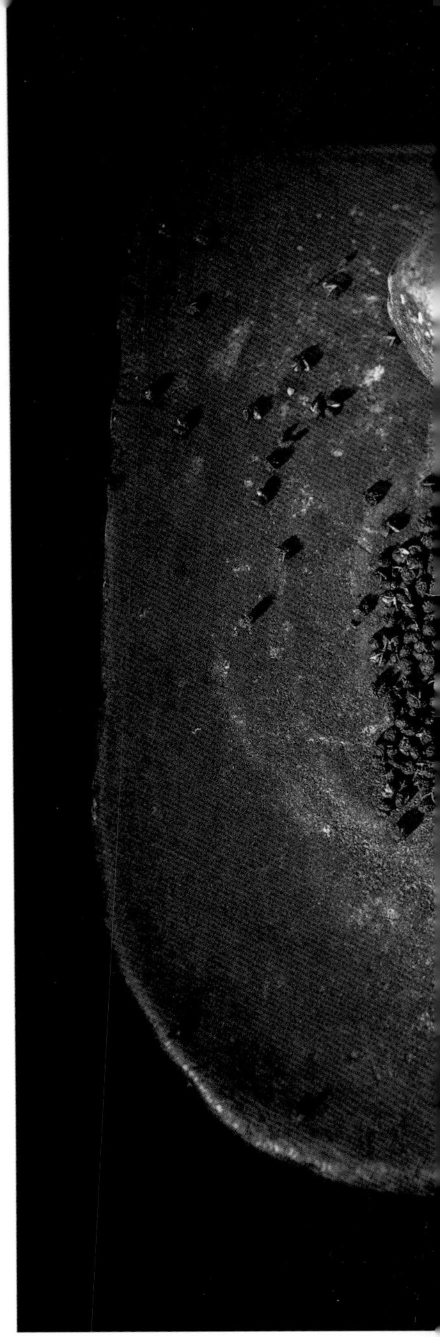

Growing up in a family composed of two different cultures, I learned to juxtapose the differing cultures of my parents through food, and understand and appreciate their contrasts. My mother's Newa community reveres alcohol and buffalo meat, which are integral to the culture and even offered to the gods. But my father's Brahmin community abstains from alcohol and buffalo meat as these are considered impure and socially unacceptable. The two communities celebrate festivals and rituals in different ways and have different food traditions.

Despite the differences, my family embraces both cultures. I grew up blending these two food cultures and traditions together. Food is the epitome of culture, and especially in Nepal, food has deep cultural and religious significance, even being the defining feature of one's cultural identity.

Nepal has over a hundred different castes and ethnicities, each with its own food culture deeply rooted within its own socio-ecological milieus. Nepal's southern plains, the Tarai, lie less than a hundred metres above sea level. To the north, spanning a couple of hundred kilometres, the hills rise to become mountains, some of which are the highest in the world. Because of its geographical variance, Nepal has a great variety of flora and fauna, including crops and animals that are raised for food, which in turn has led to variegated cuisines. Many indigenous communities in Nepal have their own distinct culinary practices that are largely defined by the environment they live in, the availability of resources, the state of the economy, and centuries of history. But little is written about the wonderful variety of food cultures across these ethnicities, and Nepali cuisine is largely represented by a handful of recipes.

In addition to indigenous practices, migration, trade, and cross-border influences have also shaped Nepali gastronomy. For centuries, Nepalis have engaged in trade between the Tibetan Plateau and the Gangetic Plains. While many of Nepal's valleys and mountains appear isolated, traditional recipes are a testament to the movement of people and cross-cultural exchanges across the Himalayas.

The Tarai's food culture relates to that of North India as they are historically, geographically, and culturally contiguous. Similarly, the food culture of Nepal's northern hinterland relates to that of Tibet. Over the years, many Tibetan and Indian communities have also migrated to Nepal, bringing along their recipes. Muslim communities, some of which came from Kashmir and Central Asia, have also blended their cuisines with local practices, customs, and ingredients. In Nepal, food practices are linked to one's religion, caste, and ethnicity. Hindus from supposedly 'upper-caste' households categorise foods according to *chokho*

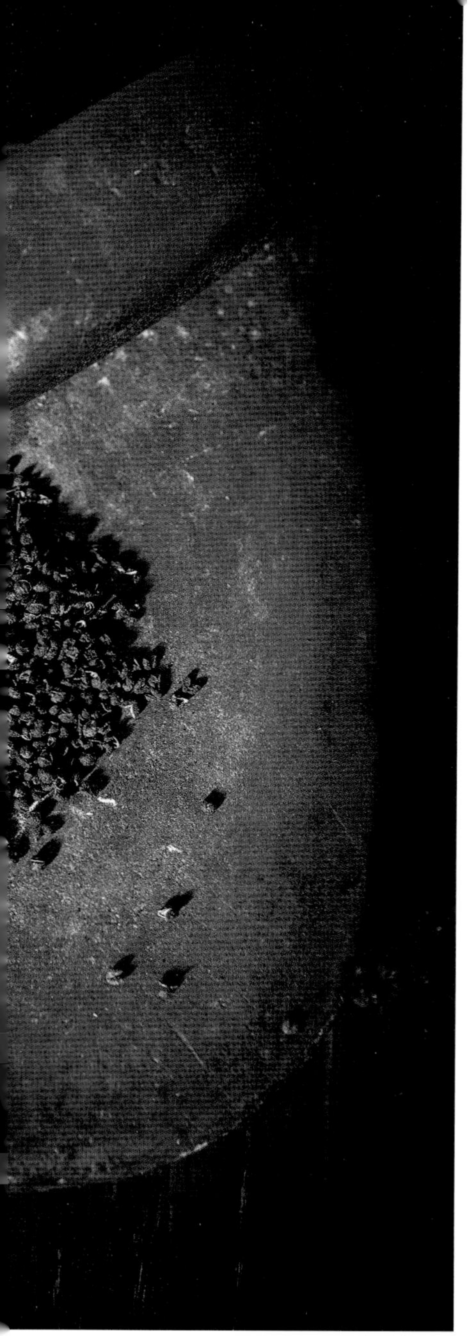

(pure) and *bitulo* (impure). For instance, *kodo* (finger millet) is considered impure and abstained during religious ceremonies. Whereas for other groups, millet is a staple and also made into alcohol that is offered to ancestral deities. Alcohol and pork consumption is a defining feature of non-Hindu ethnicities and the 'lower-caste'.

In a society stratified by caste and class, some food practices are used as a tool for discrimination and social exclusion. The upper-caste not only dictate the supremacy of their social norms but also their food culture. They look down upon those castes who eat pig and buffalo, and drink alcohol. What you eat has historically defined your class and vice versa. Dalits, the 'untouchables', are the lowest in the class hierarchy and even the water touched by them is considered impure by upper-caste Hindus.

As with most cultures around the world, the social practice of eating together is at the centre of festivities and celebrations in Nepal. Kathmandu's Newa community celebrates numerous festivals and *jatras* (chariot processions or carnivals), and for each celebration, a *bhoye* (feast) is an indispensable element. Such *bhoyes* involve the preparation of a large variety of dishes and alcoholic drinks, and are testaments to the culinary ingenuity of the Newas.

The largest Hindu festival Dashain, the Sakela festival of the Kirats, and many others festivals in Nepal are celebrations of planting and harvesting of crops that follow the monsoon cycle. In fact, monsoon shapes the ways of life in Nepal. Yomari Punhi, a Newa festival that involves eating *yomari* (a steamed rice flour cake filled with sweet molasses), and Nwagi, a festival offering the new harvest to ancestral deities before consuming in many communities, are essentially the celebrations of the crop harvest.

At times, specific delicacies are designated for specific festivals and such delicacies pay close attention to seasonally available produce. During the winter festival of Maghe Sankranti, varieties of tubers such as sweet potato, yam, and taro are consumed alongside ghee and processed jaggery in the belief that they prevent colds.

In recent decades, *daal-bhat-tarkari*, commonly referred to as *khana* (also the word for 'food'), has become a staple meal across Nepal. Daal is lentil or bean soup, *bhat* is cooked rice, and *tarkari* is cooked vegetable. The meal is at times accompanied by a meat curry and often eaten with a fermented or freshly-made achaar as relish. Rice has become so central to Nepali culture to the point where the most common colloquial greeting in the Nepali language is *bhat/khana khanu bhayo?* (have you eaten rice?). Even the weaning ritual, which celebrates an infant's first solid meal, is called *bhat-khwai* or rice-feeding. Today, rice is the major staple crop and different varieties are grown throughout Nepal below 3,000 metres.

However, many mountain communities traditionally did not eat rice as a staple. Buckwheat, barley, and naked barley once made up the daily diets of Himalayan highland communities such as the Sherpa, Tamang, and Thakali. Mid-hill communities such as the Newa, Magar, and Gurung consumed millet and maize as their primary staples. It was only in the southern plains and among the Khas-Pahadi community in the mid-hills that rice was treated with such reverence.

Barley, the oldest cultivated crop—even mentioned in the ancient Vedic scripture the *Rigveda*, composed 3,500 years ago—was once grown all over Nepal, but now is grown only in the highlands. Used as an offering to the gods, the grain holds a sacred place in Hindu and Buddhist rituals. In the plains, rice and wheat have replaced barley. The history of rice is obscure, but it might have been cultivated in the southern plains from the second millennium BC and introduced in the Kathmandu Valley by the first millennium BC. Maize, the new world crop, was introduced to the Valley in the 16th century, and apparently commonly cultivated in Nepal's hilly areas only from the mid-17th century onwards.

Apart from rice, maize, buckwheat, millet, and other grains are usually ground into flour and made into roti (unleavened flatbread) and *dhindo* (thick porridge). These starchy foods are always accompanied by a vegetable or meat curry, daal, and achaar. In the Himalayan region, *tsampa*—roasted barley or naked barley flour—is a staple and is usually eaten with *su-cha* (salty butter tea). Whole grains are used to make alcohol, which is a common practice across the country.

As rice has become more mainstream and commercially available, it has displaced other traditional and nutritious staple grains such as millet, buckwheat, barley, sorghum, and amaranth. Unfortunately, even many of the local rice varieties are being replaced by commercial varieties. Varieties like *anadi*, which is the only traditional variety of sticky rice and a cultural food of the Tharu, *marsi*, which is a cold-tolerant variety grown at an elevation of 3,000 metres in the far-west, *ghaiya*, which is a variety grown in hilly dry-lands, and *panhele* and *jethobudo*, which are two aromatic varieties grown in the western hills, were once common. Hundreds of rice varieties once existed across Nepal with some having a deep connection to particular ethnicities and regions.

One defining characteristic of Nepali cuisine is the people's inextricable links to the ecosystem they live in. Although in decline, foraging and hunting still contribute a significant portion to diets. In the hilly and mountainous regions where less fertile soil and harsh climates mean that crops cannot support residents all year round, foraging is essential to meet local needs. Locals commonly consume wild produce such as *niguro* (fiddlehead fern), *chyau* (mushroom), *tama* (bamboo shoots), and *tarul* (wild yam) when in season. Rai and Limbu communities even collect *yangben* (wild edible lichen) and cook it with pork. Seasonal wild fruits and nuts such as *dalechuk* (sea buckthorn), *ainselu* (Himalayan raspberries), *katus* (chestnut), and *okhar* (walnuts) also supplement the diet.

Before strict hunting regulations were put in place, game birds and animals such as *kalij* (pheasant), *mriga* (deer), and *bandel* (wild boar) were hunted for meat. Some hunters even ventured to higher altitudes to hunt for *ghoral* (Himalayan ghoral), *naur* (blue sheep), and *thar* (black buck).

Freshwater bodies provide food for many in the plains and hills. The food culture of the Tharus is inextricably linked to rivers, ponds, canals, and swamps. Freshwater fishes, crabs, shrimps, snails, and mussels are much-loved delicacies in the community. In the mid-hills, along with fishes, *paha* (freshwater Himalayan frogs) are delicacies of the Magars and Gurungs.

Insects, on the other hand, are only sparsely consumed now. As a child, I used to collect *barula gund* (wasp nests) for their larvae. I remember seeing the Kumal people collecting red ant eggs found in *saal* trees. Today, these insects are generally perceived as unappealing. Such indigenous foraging practices are regrettably disappearing.

Until recently, Nepalis ate meat occasionally, generally during festivals and celebrations. Usually only male animals are slaughtered for meat whereas females are kept for milk and breeding, except during religious sacrifices where young female animals are also slaughtered. Buffalo meat is of particular importance to the Newa community. Many hill communities have a variety of pork-based recipes. Yaks, mountain goats, and sheep are reared for meat in the mountainous region. *Khasi* (castrated goat) and chicken are common and consumed by most communities. Some indigenous groups traditionally ate beef, but cow slaughter was outlawed in the early 19th century by the Hindu monarchy, and it remains proscribed today.

Customarily, all animal parts are consumed by making varieties of delicacies. Almost nothing goes to waste. Mountainous communities maintain the traditional practice of making blood sausage, sometimes adding offal. Milk and dairy products such as ghee, yoghurt, and buttermilk are essential in the cuisines of Hindu Khas-Pahadi, Maithil, Sherpa, and other mountainous communities, which historically followed pastoral traditions. Hindu upper-caste and Maithil households prefer milk and dairy products over meat, and some of them completely abstain from consuming meat.

Fermenting, smoke-drying, and sun-drying are common in Nepali food culture, which probably might have come from the need to preserve food. Fermented achaars are also attempts to preserve food. Vegetables such as radish, cauliflower, *lapsi* (Nepali hog plum), bamboo shoots, and chillies are pickled and stored. This not only helps preserve perishable foods for a long time, but also develop new flavours. The Rais and Limbus ferment soybeans to make *kinema* and then dry it for later use. *Gundruk* (sun-dried fermented greens) and *masyaura* (sun-dried black lentil paste and taro leaf nuggets) are widely prepared for preserving greens for the dry season. The Thakalis sun-dry buckwheat greens and ground them to make *dhopra,* which is consumed as a soup.

While hill and mountainous communities preserve greens for the winter and dry seasons, the Tharus in the southern plains preserve greens for the monsoon season when the fields are flooded and greens are scarce. *Biriya,* made from rice or lentil flour paste and greens, is prepared by Tharu communities. *Chuk* is another commonly used preserved food, which is prepared by boiling down Nepali lemon juice, and similarly, *khudo* from sugarcane juice.

While in some communities, their economic prosperity and agricultural abundance have added richness to food; in other communities, limited crop diversity and the necessity for preservation have led to the development of unique delicacies and flavours.

A wide variety of spices, herbs, and flavouring ingredients used in cooking also reflects the richness of Nepali flavours. Mustard oil, ghee, and sometimes preserved animal fat have been used as cooking mediums and flavouring ingredients since ancient times. But today, the use of industrially processed sunflower and soybean oil is widespread. Roasted mustard oil, known as *buchika* in the Newa language, is a typical flavouring ingredient in Newa kitchens, especially to flavour achaars.

Spices such as garlic, ginger, onion, coriander, cumin, turmeric, and chilli are commonly used across Nepal, but there are also many lesser-known spices and flavouring ingredients distinctive to communities or regions. The Sherpas use the whey dregs of buttermilk, known as *serkam.* They also ferment *serkam* to make *somar*, and milk cream to make *shosim,* both of which add a sharp pungent flavour to soups and achaars.

In Nepal's western parts, *bhang* (hemp seeds) is widely used to make achaar. The Tharus in the eastern Tarai use *aalash* (flaxseeds) to flavour curries and achaars. *Timmur* and *jimbu* (aromatic wild Himalayan allium) are among the important flavouring ingredients in Thakali cuisine, and also commonly used by hill communities. Among the Kirats, burnt ash from a rooster's inner feathers is used as flavouring to make a delicacy known as *wachipa* or *wamrik.*

Nepali cuisine is characterised by the one quality that distinguishes almost every facet of Nepali life: its diversity. With wide geographic variance, ethnic diversity, rich culture and heritage, Nepali food culture is intricately and extraordinarily unique. Nepal has managed to carve out a unique niche for itself, borrowing not just from its neighbours, but also cultures farther afield.

As the identity, culture, religion, ethnicity, and beliefs of the communities are intrinsically connected to food, it is imperative to understand and preserve Nepal's food culture.

Newa Cuisine

KATHMANDU'S SUMPTUOUS FEASTS FIT FOR THE GODS

My mother's Newa ancestors migrated out of the Kathmandu Valley possibly in the late 18th century, some time after it was invaded by the expanding Gorkha kingdom. They moved west to the hills of Tanahun and, with time, have forgotten some culinary practices while adopting new ones from their neighbouring communities. I discovered the richness of Newa cuisine only after I moved to Kathmandu in 2003. In a local Newa eatery, tucked away in the ancient meandering alleys of Basantapur, I discovered the savoury delights of *wo* (lentil pancake), *chatamari* (rice flour pancake) topped with meat and egg, and *chhoyla* (barbecued buffalo meat mixed with spices).

The Newa people (also known as the Newars) have lived in the Kathmandu Valley for millennia. Since ancient times, the Valley was prosperous, thriving on its fertile lands which yielded an abundance of crops, and on trade with Tibet and India. The Valley's prosperity and cross-cultural influence are reflected in its food culture, extravagant festivities, and beautiful architecture.

The Valley's fertile plains, an ancient lake bed, fed by rivers and irrigation systems, were ideal for rice cultivation. Kathmandu today is built on its once abundant paddy fields. Rice is thus central to Newa cuisine, and the culinary ingenuity of the Newas is reflected in the versatility of this grain as an essential ingredient. *Baji* (beaten rice) is a staple food prepared by soaking, steaming, roasting, and then milling un-husked rice. Rice is fermented to brew *thwon* (fermented alcoholic rice drink) and distilled to make *aila* (rice liquor). Both beaten rice and alcoholic rice drinks hold an important place in Newa culture, as they are prerequisites for every festival and religious and cultural occasion. They are offered to the gods and also taken back as an offering from the gods. *Yomari*, a special confection consisting of steamed rice flour dough filled with *chaku* (jaggery taffy) and roasted sesame seed grounds, or *khuwa* (evaporated milk solids), is specifically prepared during the Yomari Punhi festival, a celebration of the rice harvest.

Newa food culture would be incomplete without the mention of the special place that (male) buffalo meat, colloquially referred to as 'buff' in English, occupies. While historic records are sparse, the practice of rearing buffaloes in the Valley existed as early as 700 BC during the Mahisapala period. Concerning the consumption of buffaloes, legends go back to the 14th century, but it might be a much older practice. In 1324 AD, the Karnat dynasty king Harisimha Deva fled to Nepal after the Islamic invasion destabilised his kingdom in India. Deva and his soldiers nearly died of starvation while fleeing the invaders. In desperation, he invoked his protector goddess Taleju for help. The goddess then appeared to the king in a vision and instructed him to sacrifice the first beast he saw at dawn. The next morning, the king came across a wild buffalo and offered it to Taleju, who then permitted the king and his people to consume the animal upon sacrifice. Harisimha Deva's descendants later came to rule Kathmandu and never forgot the animal that had saved their lives.

The buffalo is thus sacrificed to the gods, and there are no festivals and celebrations without its meat. Buffalo meat is employed in a variety of ways: curry, stew, soup, raw minced, barbecued, and sun-dried. Almost every part of the buffalo is transformed into a unique delicacy: bone marrow wrapped in tripe to make *sapumicha;* leg and head parts cooked into soft gelatinous *takha;* lungs stuffed with rice batter to make *swan puka;* blood steamed to make *chohi;* and spinal marrow fried to make *tisya.*

In the Kathmandu Valley, festivities and celebrations begin with Gathamugha, a festival just after planting season in August, and last until Sithi Nakha, a festival in June next year, before the farmers head back to the fields with the onset of monsoon. The three main cities of the Valley host extravagant *jatras* (chariot processions and festivals), like Yenya (Indra jatra) in Kathmandu, Bungya Dya (Rato Machhindranath Jatra) in Patan, and Biskah Jatra in Bhaktapur. These celebrations are accompanied by a *bhoye*, a traditional communal feast, with a plethora of food and plenty of alcoholic drinks made from rice. For Yenya, an elaborated religious street festival in Kathmandu, the community makes a cornucopian display of *samay-baji* at each *chowk* or neighbourhood. Shaped into a mound, the display consists of numerous dishes that symbolise auspiciousness: beaten rice, lentils, buffalo meat, black soybeans, egg, fish, and greens. Alcohol, fruits, and sweets are also included in the display. The entire *samay-baji* is later distributed amongst participants as *prasad,* a gift from the gods.

Numerous Newa festivals revolve around the preparation and consumption of special dishes. For instance, *kwanti,* a hearty soup consisting of sprouting mixed beans, is eaten during Gunhu/Kwanti Punhi, a full moon day festival on the tenth month of the Newa lunar calendar; ghee, *chaku* (jaggery taffy), sesame seeds balls, and tubers are eaten during Ghya-Chaku Sanhlu, a winter solstice festival; and *chatamari* (rice flour roti) during Sithi Nakha, a festival marking the beginning of monsoon.

Newa cuisine, however, did not develop in isolation; it is a rich and complex tradition that also borrows from the north and south. As occupational merchants from Kathmandu travelled to the plains of India and the plateaus of Tibet, they brought back dishes, cooking styles, and ingredients to Newa kitchens. The momo, perhaps the most popular of Nepali foods, was brought back from Lhasa in the 17th century, and from where it spread across Nepal and into the hills of India. These dumplings, a version of the Chinese *jiaozi,* were adapted to local tastes with the use of buffalo meat and local spices. Similarly, the merchant Tuladhar clan has maintained a tradition of drinking *su-cha* (Tibetan butter tea) during communal gatherings. Sweets, on the other hand, are a reflection of Indian influence. Newa sweets such as halwa (dense confection made from semolina flour, ghee, and sugar), laddu (sphere-shaped sweet of sesame seeds or flour and jaggery), and *jeri* (spiral shaped deep-fried confection made from flour batter and soaked in sugar syrup) came from India.

The richness of Newa heritage is testament to the long history of its civilisation and its intercultural exchanges across the Himalayas. Kathmandu had certainly gone through many political and social changes, but food has always bound the community together, manifesting as a distinct marker of Newa cultural identity.

Chhoyla: Buffalo meat barbecued over rice straw flame, and mixed with spices and roasted mustard oil.

Baji: Flat crispy beaten rice flakes.

Gwaramari: Savoury deep-fried balls prepared from lightly fermented wheat flour dough.

Yomari: Sweet steamed rice flour confection/cake typically with sesame seeds and *chaku* (jaggery taffy) filling.

Lonchamari: Steamed rice flour and sugar mixed dough.

Lakhamari: Deep-fried sweets made from rice and lentil flour, sugar, and ghee.

Wo: Savoury lentil pancakes, sometimes topped with minced meat and/or egg.

Chatamari: Thin crispy savoury rice flour pancake/*roti,* sometimes topped with minced meat, vegetables, and/or egg.

Momo/Momocha: Steamed dumplings filled with minced meat and spices, typically served with tomato achaar.

Dyagula: Buff stew with aromatic spices.

Meekwa: Fenugreek seeds and small field peas soup.

Bula/Kakwa: Stew prepared from remaining dregs of *thwon* (rice wine) and buffalo bones, cartilage, and bone marrow.

Aalu Chhon (Aalu-tama): Tangy and spicy *tama* (fermented bamboo shoots) soup with potatoes and black-eyed beans.

Paunkwa: Thick sour and spicy soup prepared from *lapsi*.

Kwanti: Soup prepared traditionally from mixed sprouted beans and lentils.

Bhyata ken: Winter curry of sun-dried broad leaf mustard greens, soybeans, and rice grits.

Aalu wala: Boiled potato salad or achaar mixed with spices.

Musya wala: Roasted soybeans mixed with spices.

Takha and Sanyakhuna: Gelatinous dish prepared by cooking the leg and head meat of a buffalo for several hours (the latter is prepared by adding smoked fish, chilli powder, and citrus juice).

Kachila: Raw minced buffalo meat spiced with ginger, garlic, chilli, salt, and roasted mustard oil.

Janla: Raw tender buffalo skin mixed with spices.

Chohi: Steamed cake made from the clear liquid that has been separated from buffalo blood and bone marrow.

Sapumicha: Deep-fried tripe stuffed with bone marrow.

Samay-baji: An important religious and cultural platter eaten during festivals and celebrations consisting of a set of food items: *baji*, *wo*, *chhoyla*, *aalu wala*, *musya wala*, *khen* (boiled egg), *sanya* (smoked fish), *waucha* (stir-fried greens).

Dhau: Yoghurt.

Thwon: Rice wine (sometimes prepared from beaten rice). *Hyaun thwon* is red colour fermented rice wine, sometime flavoured with roasted green chillies.

Aila: Distilled hard liquor extracted from fermented rice.

WO

Savory lentil pancake

Wo is a savoury lentil pancake prepared traditionally from black lentil paste. Nowadays, mung beans are also used. It is prepared by the Newa community on almost all special occasions and festivals, especially as an essential item in *samay-baji*, an auspicious platter of foods. In Newa eateries, it is also served with egg and/or minced meat toppings.

2 cups black lentils
2 tablespoons garlic paste
2 tablespoons ginger paste
4–5 tablespoons roasted mustard oil, if not available, use regular vegetable oil
Salt as per taste

Topping, Optional
1 cup minced buffalo meat or meat of choice
1 teaspoon ginger paste
1 teaspoon garlic paste
½ teaspoon turmeric powder
1 teaspoon vegetable oil
Salt as per taste
Eggs

*makes about 10–12 *wo*

Wash and soak the black lentils overnight.

Massage the soaked lentils using palms to separate the outer black layer. Then wash the lentils several times to remove the layers. It is not necessary to remove the layers completely.

Drain the water and put the black lentils in a food-processer or use a large mortar and pestle. Add the ginger and garlic paste, some salt, and a tablespoon of roasted mustard oil. Grind them together until it forms a fine paste.

Heat a thick-base pan over medium heat. Drizzle a teaspoon of roasted mustard oil to grease the pan. When the pan is hot enough, take a handful or a ladle of black lentil paste mixture and spread it evenly in the pan using the hand or the back of the ladle, forming a round shape. Cook both sides for 3–4 minutes. The *wo* is ready.

To make *wo* with toppings

First, mix the minced meat and all the spices together.

After adding the lentil paste mixture into the pan, spread it into a round shape, and spread 2–3 tablespoons of the minced meat on top and crack an egg in the centre. Cook it for about 3–4 minutes or until the lower part is light brown. Drizzle a teaspoon of roasted mustard oil over the pancake and flip it using a spatula. Cook it for another 4–5 minutes.

Serve it hot. *Wo* is often served in Newa eateries with a buff stew *(dyagula)* soup or a simple tomato achaar.

CHATAMARI

Thin rice flour roti

Chatamari, a traditional specialty of the Newa community, is a plain rice flour roti or crepe. Nowadays, a variety of ingredients such as potatoes, beans, eggs, and minced meat are used as toppings to make *chatamari* more flavourful and filling. It is commonly eaten during the Sithi Nakha festival and the annual Dewali festival when the ancestral deity of the family is worshipped.

Roti
1 cup rice flour
3–4 tablespoons roasted mustard oil

Toppings
2–3 medium-sized boiled potatoes and a half cup of soaked and boiled black-eyed peas or 100 gm minced buffalo meat
1 teaspoon ginger paste
1 teaspoon garlic paste
½ teaspoon cumin and coriander powder mix
½ teaspoon red chilli powder or green chillies, finely chopped
½ teaspoon turmeric powder
2–3 tomatoes, finely sliced
A small handful of coriander leaves, finely chopped
1 teaspoon vegetable oil
Salt as per taste
Eggs, optional

*makes 6–8 *chatamari*

Mix a cup of rice flour with about one and a half cup of water in a bowl and make a batter.

In a bowl, mix together the mashed boiled potatoes and black-eyed peas (for vegetarian) or minced meat (for non-vegetarian) with the ginger paste, garlic paste, and cumin, coriander, red chilli, and turmeric powder, vegetable oil, and salt to make toppings.

Heat a thick-base pan over medium heat and grease it very lightly with some vegetable oil. When the pan is hot enough, spread a ladle of the rice batter thinly with the back of a spatula (or by tilting the pan), giving the roti a round shape. Spread 3–4 tablespoons of the toppings on the roti and crack an egg on top (optional). Then drizzle some roasted mustard oil and spread some finely sliced tomatoes and chopped fresh coriander leaves on top. Cook over medium heat with the lid on for about 10–12 minutes.

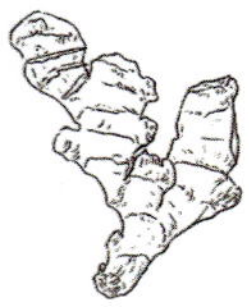

MOMO-CHA

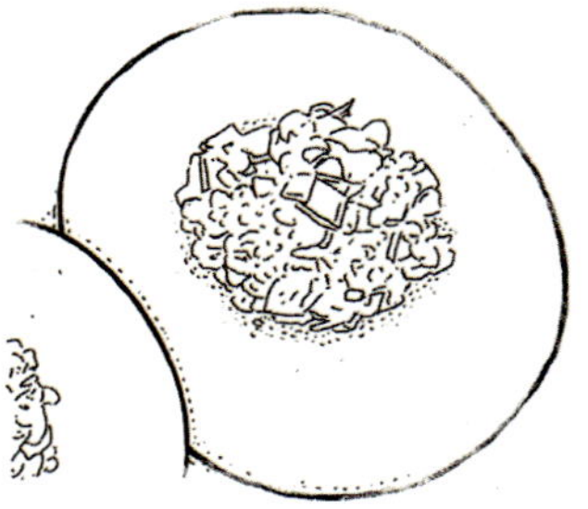

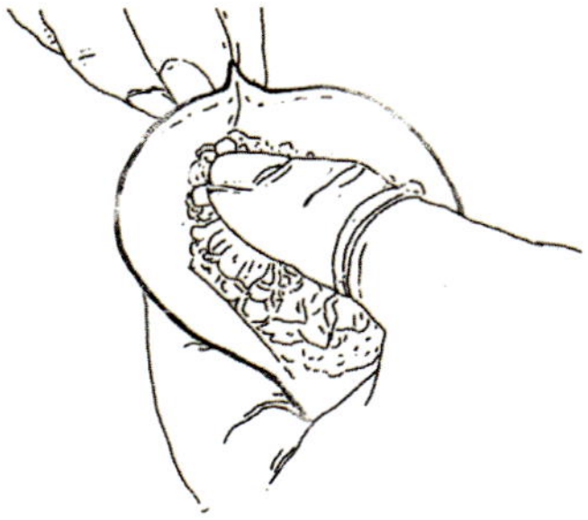

Buffalo meat dumplings

Momo is one of the most popular foods in Nepal, especially in Kathmandu and urban areas. The momo is a dumpling filled with minced meat (or vegetables) mixed with spices and served with achaar, generally made from tomatoes. The *momo-cha* is a smaller variant of the dumplings with a buffalo meat filling and served with soupy *jhol* achaar made from sesame seeds and soybeans. It was brought to the Kathmandu Valley from Tibet by Newa traders and has been adapted to local tastes using buffalo meat and local spices.

Momo wrappers
1 cup plain wheat flour
½ cup water
1 tablespoon vegetable oil

Momo filling
500 gm minced buff, including some fat or bone marrow
2 medium-sized onions, very finely chopped
1–2 spring onions, finely chopped
1 teaspoon ginger paste
1 teaspoon garlic paste
1 teaspoon cumin and coriander powder mix
½ teaspoon black pepper powder
½ teaspoon cinnamon powder
½ teaspoon turmeric powder
A handful of coriander leaves, finely chopped
2 tablespoons vegetable oil
Salt as per taste

***Jhol* achaar**
4–5 tablespoons sesame seeds
3–4 tablespoons soybeans
2–3 medium-sized tomatoes
2–3 garlic cloves, roughly chopped
½ thumb-sized ginger, roughly chopped
2–3 tablespoons *lapsi* powder, alternatively use a lemon or lime
1 teaspoon red chilli powder
A handful of coriander leaves, finely chopped
Salt as per taste

*serves 3–4 people

Add a cup of plain wheat flour, a tablespoon of vegetable oil, and about half a cup of water in a bowl, and mix them together to make dough for momo wrappings. Add some more flour if the dough is too soft or some water if it is a bit firm. Knead the dough. Leave it covered for 15–20 minutes with a slightly moist cloth or in an airtight container to avoid drying.

Add the minced meat with some fat or bone marrow, finely chopped onions, spring onions, and all the spices in a large bowl to make the filling. Mix them together by hand or with a spoon. Fat and bone marrow make the meat juicy and flavourful.

For the momo wraps, take small amounts of dough and roll them in between your palms to make small marble-sized balls. Dust a rolling pin with flour and roll the balls into thin circular wraps with a diameter of about 5–6 centimetres.

Place a tablespoon of the filling in the middle of the wrap and make a pleat. There are multiple ways to wrap the momo. Refer to the illustrations for instructions. Wrapping requires practice.

Grease a steamer with vegetable oil before placing the momo in it. This will keep them from sticking to the bottom. Steam for about 12–15 minutes.

For the soupy *jhol* achaar, separately roast the sesame seeds, soybeans and tomatoes in a pan. Place these, along with all the remaining ingredients and spices (except for the coriander leaves), salt, and *lapsi* powder (or some lemon juice), in a grinder or a mortar and pestle. Grind them together until they turn into a fine paste. Add about two and a half cups of water into the mixture and blend. Add more salt if required. Garnish with the finely chopped fresh coriander leaves.

CHHOYLA

Barbecued meat with spices and roasted mustard oil

Chhoyla means barbecued or roasted meat, which is flavoured with raw ginger and garlic and roasted mustard oil. This popular Newa dish is an essential item in *samay-baji*. Traditionally, buffalo meat is barbecued medium-rare over a rice straw flame, which helps to create a black smoky outer layer while keeping the inside meat juicy. This type of *chhoyla* is known as *haku chhoyla*. A variant is made by boiling meat, which is known as *mana chhoyla*. One can also prepare *chhoyla* by searing meat over charcoal or firewood or on a pan.

500 gm lean buffalo meat
1–2 garlic leaves
1 tablespoon ginger paste
1 tablespoon garlic paste
1 tablespoon red chilli powder
Salt as per taste

Tempering spices
2 tablespoons roasted mustard oil
1 teaspoon fenugreek seeds
1 teaspoon turmeric powder

*serves 3–4 people

Cut the meat into long stripes a few centimetres thick. Barbecue the meat until medium rare over rice straw, charcoal or firewood flame. Let it rest for about five minutes as this helps to keep the meat juicy.

Cut the barbecued meat into small bite-sized pieces and transfer to a large bowl. Add the chopped garlic leaves, ginger and garlic paste, red chilli powder, and salt.

Heat about two tablespoons of roasted mustard oil in a small saucepan, and temper the fenugreek seeds and turmeric powder. Pour them over the meat immediately. Mix well and the *chhoyla* is ready. *Chhoyla* is generally eaten together with beaten rice or as part of *samay-baji*.

KWANTI

Mixed bean sprout soup

Kwanti, a very nutritious dish high in protein and fiber, is relished by the Newas and nowadays, as well as other communities of Nepal. Typically prepared from a mixture of nine different beans, *kwanti*, according to local belief, improves digestion and bolsters the body's immunity against seasonal ailments. *Kwanti* means hot soup in the Newa language. *Kwanti* beans generally include black lentil, chickpea, rice bean, black-eyed bean, soy bean, white bean, garden pea, broad bean, and mung bean. Sometimes, meat or momos are added to the *kwanti* soup.

This festive delicacy is especially prepared on Gunu Punhi or Kwanti Punhi, the full moon festival in August, which is towards the end of the monsoon season. It is essentially consumed to nourish and rejuvenate the body after months of hard work in the paddy fields. On the particular day, Hindus observe Janai Purnima by tying a sacred thread around their wrist, a ritual that is believed to protect the wearer from bad spirits.

1 cup *kwanti* beans
1 thumb-sized ginger
3–4 garlic cloves
2–3 bay leaves (*tej patta*)
2–3 tablespoons vegetable oil
Salt as per taste

Tempering spices
1–2 tablespoon ghee/butter
½ teaspoon ajwain (*jwano*)
½ teaspoon fenugreek seeds
1–2 dry red chillies
1 tablespoon cumin and coriander powder mix
½ teaspoon turmeric powder

*serves 2–3 people

Soak a cup of *kwanti* beans overnight, drain the water, and loosely wrap or cover them with a damp muslin cloth for two days for them to sprout.

Wash the sprouts and place them in a pressure cooker. Add three cups of water, smashed ginger and garlic, bay leaves, salt, and a tablespoon of vegetable oil. Put the lid on and boil them over low-medium heat for around 15–20 minutes (4–5 whistles). If you are using a regular pot, cook the beans for a longer time, over an hour. Turn off the heat and leave the pressure cooker to cool on its own.

Take the lid off the pressure cooker and add about two cups of hot water or more. Give it a good stir and boil for another 5–8 minutes over low-medium heat.

Temper spices by frying them over low heat. Heat 1–2 tablespoons of ghee in a small pan, and add the finely sliced garlic, dry red chillies, fenugreek seeds, and *jwano*. As soon as the seeds start to pop, add the turmeric and cumin-coriander powder. Turn off the heat and pour the tempered spices into the soup. Garnish the soup with the fresh coriander leaves.

MEEKWA

Fenugreek sprout soup

Meekwa is a traditional Newa soup prepared from fenugreek sprouts. It is one of the many Newa dishes eaten during *bhoye*, and served almost at the end. Fenugreek, known as *methi* in Nepali and *mee* in Newa, is a commonly used spice in Nepali cuisine. The soup has a tinge of bitterness from the fenugreek seeds.

200 gm fenugreek seeds
200 gm field peas, optional
1 medium-sized onion
2–3 garlic cloves
1 thumb-sized ginger
1 tablespoon cumin and coriander powder mix
1 teaspoon red chilli powder
½ teaspoon turmeric powder
2–3 tablespoons vegetable oil
Salt as per taste

Tempering spices
1–2 tablespoons vegetable oil
½ teaspoon turmeric powder

*serves 3–4 people

Soak the fenugreek seeds and field peas (optional) overnight in separate bowls. Wash the soaked fenugreek seeds a few times to temper their bitterness. The soup is generally prepared from sprouted fenugreek seeds and peas, so leave them covered with a muslin cloth for a day or two to sprout.

Boil three cups of water in a pot. Add the soaked fenugreek seeds, peas, finely sliced onion, smashed garlic cloves and ginger, cumin and coriander powder, red chilli powder, and salt. Continue boiling over medium heat with the lid on until the fenugreek seeds and the peas are cooked through. This should take about 20–25 minutes. Add more water if required and bring it to a boil.

In a small saucepan, heat 1–2 tablespoons of vegetable oil to temper the spices. Add the turmeric and turn the heat off. Pour immediately into the soup.

AALU CHHON

Fermented bamboo shoot, potato, and black-eyed bean soup

Commonly known as *aalu tama* in Nepali, this spicy and tangy soup is made from potatoes, fermented bamboo shoots *(chhon)*, and black-eyed beans. When bamboo shoots are bountiful during the monsoon season, they are preserved by fermentation. Fermented bamboo shoots add a peculiar tangy flavour to the dish. It is enjoyed all year round and usually eaten with beaten rice, cooked rice, or *wo*.

3–4 medium-sized potatoes
1 cup fermented bamboo shoots
½ cup black-eyed beans
2–3 medium-sized tomatoes
1 medium-sized onion
1 tablespoon ginger paste
1 tablespoon garlic paste
2–3 green chillies
1 tablespoon cumin and coriander powder mix
1 teaspoon red chilli powder
1 teaspoon turmeric powder
1 teaspoon fenugreek seeds
1 teaspoon cumin seeds
2–3 tablespoons vegetable oil
Salt as per taste
Fresh coriander leaves for garnish

*serves 3–4 people

Soak the black-eyed beans overnight. Boil the soaked beans and potatoes separately until cooked. Peel the potatoes after they cool down and cut them into bite-size pieces.

Heat about 2–3 tablespoons of vegetable oil in a cooking pot over medium heat, and fry cumin and fenugreek seeds. Add the finely chopped onion and ginger-garlic paste. Cook until they turn light brown. Then add two whole green chillies and turmeric powder.

Add a cup of fermented bamboo shoots and fry them together for a couple of minutes. Add the chopped tomatoes and cook for about 3–4 minutes until they become soft. Add the boiled potatoes, black-eyed beans, salt, and cumin, coriander, and red chilli powder. Cook for about 4–5 minutes, stirring occasionally.

Pour about 3–4 cups of water, preferably hot, into the mixture and cook for about 15–20 minutes over low heat. Garnish with some chopped fresh coriander leaves at the end.

PAUNKWA

Lapsi soup

Paunkwa is a hot and sour soup prepared from *lapsi* (Nepali hog plum). It is served towards the end of a long sumptuous *bhoye* just before serving the *sisabusa* (mixture of radish, cucumber, and peas) and yoghurt. After a heavy feast, it is consumed to ease the digestion and cleanse the palate.

400 gm *lapsi*
1 teaspoon fenugreek seeds
1 tablespoon *bire nun* (Himalayan black rock salt)
½ teaspoon *hing* (asafoetida), optional
1 teaspoon red chilli powder
1–2 dry red chillies
1 teaspoon turmeric powder
2 tablespoons vegetable oil

*serves for 5–6 people

Cook the *lapsi* in a pot with about two cups of water for around 20–25 minutes or until the skin ruptures. They can also be cooked in a pressure cooker over medium heat for about 4–5 whistles.

After they have cooled, mash them with the hands. Remove the pit and skin of the *lapsi*. Then add about 2–3 cups of water into the mashed pulp and bring to a boil. Add the rock salt, asafoetida, and red chilli powder. Cook on low heat for another 10–12 minutes.

In a small saucepan, heat two tablespoons of vegetable oil, and fry the fenugreek seeds, dry red chillies, and turmeric powder. Pour the mixture into the soup immediately. Give it a good stir and serve in a small bowl.

Do not throw away the skin of the *lapsi*. It can be sun-dried and ground into an achaar.

DYAGULA

Buff stew or curry

Dyagula, which means cooked meat, is a stew or curry prepared by cooking buffalo meat, including bone-in and skin-on meat, with spices. One of the key flavouring ingredients of the *dyagula* is ginger, and the dish is generally cooked with more than the usual amount of ginger. It is traditionally cooked in a thick-base narrow-neck pot known as *kasaundi,* or a larger one usually made of copper known as *phowsi* during large feasts. Nowadays, a pressure cooker is commonly used for faster cooking. At home, we eat it with rice or beaten rice and *selroti* (deep-fried rice flour roti) during Mohani Nakha or Dashain.

1 kg buffalo meat, with bone-in and skin-on meat cut into bite-sized pieces
1 large onion, finely sliced
3–4 tomatoes, roughly sliced
3–4 bay leaves
1 teaspoon fenugreek seeds
2–3 dry red chillies
1 tablespoon cumin seeds
1 tablespoon coriander seeds
3–4 garlic cloves
2 thumb-sized ginger
1 teaspoon turmeric powder
Salt as per taste
3–4 tablespoons vegetable oil
A handful of fresh coriander leaves

*serves 4–5 people

Grind the cumin seeds, coriander seeds, garlic, ginger, and dry red chillies, adding about a tablespoon of water to make a spice paste.

Heat about 3–4 tablespoons of vegetable oil in a pot over medium heat. When the oil is hot enough, add the bay leaves, fenugreek seeds, and the finely sliced onion. When the onions turn soft and light brown, add the turmeric powder, stir, and add meat. Increase the heat and fry the meat for about 8–10 minutes until it is light brown.

Then add the spice paste and salt. Give it a good stir and cook for another 3–4 minutes or until the raw smell of the spices disappears. Add tomatoes and cook for another 3–4 minutes with the lid on or until the tomatoes melt.

Add 3–4 cups of water and cook over low-medium heat for 15–20 minutes with the lid on. If using a pressure cooker, cook for about two whistles. Add more water if required and bring it to a boil.

Turn off the heat and garnish the *dyagula* with the fresh coriander leaves.

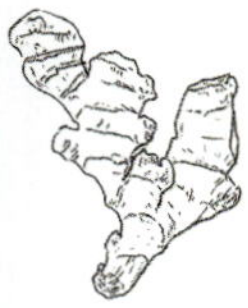

KAKWA

Soup made from dregs of fermented rice and buffalo meat

The dregs that remain after the extraction of the fermented alcoholic rice drink *thwon* and the less prized parts of the buffalo like bone-in meat, spleen, and bone marrow are cooked together to make the delicious *kakwa* soup. Also known as *bulla*, *kaji-kwa* or simply *ka*, the soup is traditionally cooked in a *phwosi* for several hours, making it thick and creamy.

Best enjoyed during winter, *kakwa* is prepared during feasts and Mohani Nakha or Dashain. In the Jyapu community, it is an essential food item for the first death anniversary ritual and even offered to the gods.

1 kg buffalo bone-in meat including bone marrow
½ litre dregs of fermented rice *(ka)*
3–4 bay leaves
1 large thumb-sized ginger
4–5 garlic cloves
1 medium-sized onion
1 teaspoon red chilli powder
1 teaspoon turmeric powder
1 tablespoon cumin and coriander powder
2–3 tablespoons mustard oil
Salt as per taste

*serves 5–6 people

Cut the bone-in meat and bone marrow into small bite-sized pieces. Mash the dregs of fermented rice into a paste using your hand or spatula. Chop an onion and make a paste of ginger and garlic.

Put a large pot over medium heat and add the mustard oil. When the oil is hot, add the bay leaves, chopped onion, and ginger-garlic paste. When the chopped onion and paste turn light brown, add the meat and turmeric. Cook the meat for about 10–12 minutes and then add the bone marrow. Cook for another 5–6 minutes while occasionally stirring. Then add the cumin, coriander, and red chilli powder, salt, and dregs of fermented rice. Stir again and add 3–4 litres of water. Lower the heat and cook for about three hours stirring occasionally until the soup becomes thick and creamy. *Kakwa* is best served hot.

AALU LAPSIKO ACHAAR

Potato and lapsi achaar

This sour spicy boiled potato and *lapsi* achaar is commonly prepared during the festivals between September and December, when the *lapsi* is in season. One can also add radish and green peas to the achaar. *Lapsi* is widely used as a souring agent and flavouring ingredient in Newa cuisine. The Newas also make a variety of achaars, fruit leather, and soups from the fruit. It is also dried and used when the fresh fruit is not available.

500 gm potatoes
5–6 fresh ripe *lapsi*
2 tablespoons sesame seeds
1 teaspoon *timmur*
1 teaspoon cumin powder
1 teaspoon red chilli powder
2–3 green chillies
2–3 garlic cloves
A handful of coriander leaves
1–2 green garlic leaves, optional
Salt as per taste

Tempering spices

2 tablespoons roasted mustard oil - or any other vegetable oil
2–3 dry red chillies
1 teaspoon fenugreek seeds
1 teaspoon turmeric powder

*serves 3–4 people

Boil the *lapsi* with half a cup of water for about 12–15 minutes or until the skin ruptures. *Lapsi* is extremely sour, but also has a little sweetness. If you can't find fresh *lapsi*, you can use dry *lapsi* powder.

Boil the potatoes until they are cooked. Leave them to cool, and peel off the skin.

Break or cut the boiled potatoes into small cubes and put them in a large mixing bowl. Add the chopped green chillies, coriander leaves, garlic leaves, and finely sliced garlic.

Remove the stone and skin of the boiled *lapsi* using your hands, and add the soft flesh to the mixture. If you are using dry *lapsi* powder, soak 1–2 tablespoons of the powder in two tablespoons of water for a couple of minutes and add to the mixture.

Lightly roast the sesame seeds and *timmur*, grind them, and add to the potatoes. Add the cumin and red chilli powder and salt as per taste.

To temper the spices, heat a small saucepan and add about two tablespoons of roasted mustard oil. When the oil is hot enough, add the fenugreek seeds and dry red chillies. When the seeds turn brown, add the turmeric powder. Turn off the heat immediately and pour the oil over the achaar mix.

Add 2–3 tablespoons of water to make the achaar moist. Mix them all together by hand or with a spoon. Garnish the mixture with some coriander leaves. This sour spicy potato achaar can be eaten as a side dish with *daal-bhat-tarkari*, roti, beaten rice, or as a part of *samay-baji*.

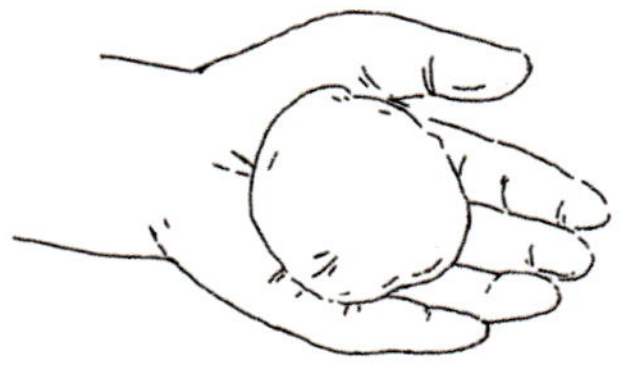
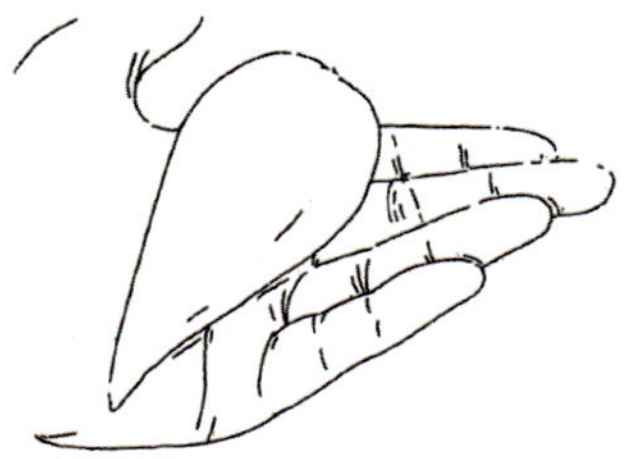
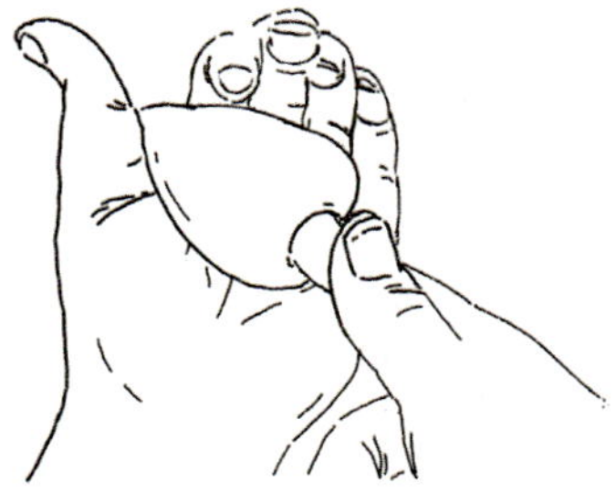

YOMARI

Steamed rice cake with jaggery taffy and sesame seed filling

Yomari is a steamed rice flour cake or confection filled with *chaku* (jaggery taffy) and sesame seed grounds. The rice flour used in making the *yomari* is of *taichin* rice, a glutinous rice variety grown in the Kathmandu Valley, which is also used for making beaten rice. *Khuwa* (evaporated milk solids) with shredded coconut is also used as a filling instead of *chaku. Chaku* is prepared by cooking sugarcane jaggery until dark brown and aerated by pulling and stretching, giving it a gloss and a chewy texture. There is also a savoury variety of *yomari* with a filling of black lentil paste.

In the Newa language, *ya* means liked or loved and *mari* means roti. This delicacy is eaten during the Yomari Punhi festival, which marks the end of the rice harvest season and falls on the full moon night in the month of *Poush* or December. The inscription in the the Kathmandu Valley shows that the festival was celebrated as early as the 6th century, during the Lichchhavi period. On this day, the Newas of the Kathmandu Valley worship Annapurna, the goddess of grains, and children go around the neighbourhood singing and asking for *yomari*:

> *Yomari chuamu, ukiya dune hamu*
> *byumha lyase, mabyumha buri kuti*
>
> (Inside the pointed *yomari* are sesame seeds
> who offers *yomari* is a young woman, who doesn't is an old lady)

Yomari is also prepared during the even-numbered birthday celebration of children until they reach the age of twelve. A garland of *yomari*—made with the number of *yomari* reflecting the age of the child—worn around the neck. Parents also feed *yomari* to pregnant daughters.

2 cups rice flour
200 gm *chaku*
½ cup roasted sesame seeds grounds
2–3 tablespoons vegetable oil

*makes about 8–10 *yomaris*

Break the *chaku* into small pieces so that it can melt easily. Put the *chaku* pieces in a saucepan and add about half a cup of water. Heat the pan on low heat until the *chaku* melts completely. Then add the sesame seeds grounds and a tablespoon of rice flour. Cook over low heat for 2–3 minutes, stirring continuously until it acquires a thick honey-like consistency.

(For a *khuwa* filling, mix *khuwa,* sugar, and finely grated/shredded coconut. To make a *mya yomari* filling, make a paste of soaked black lentils, add ginger and garlic paste, and salt, and mix together.)

For the *yomari* dough, place two cups of *taichin* rice flour in a large bowl and add about a cup of warm water. Mix them together by hand and knead until the dough is soft. Leave the dough for about half an hour by covering it with a moist cloth to prevent it from drying.

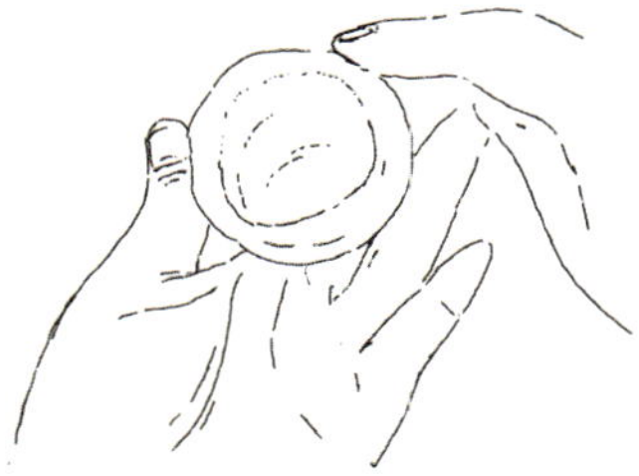

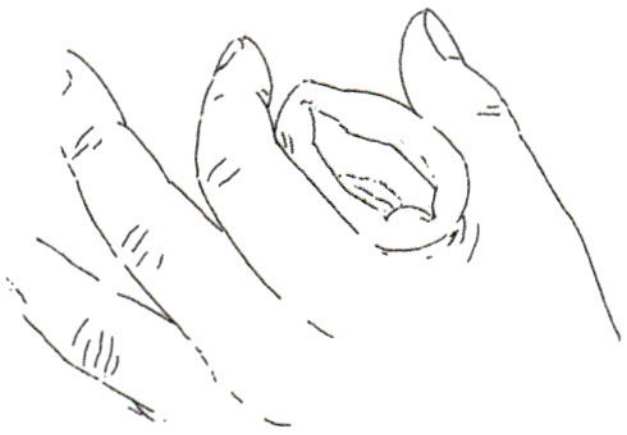

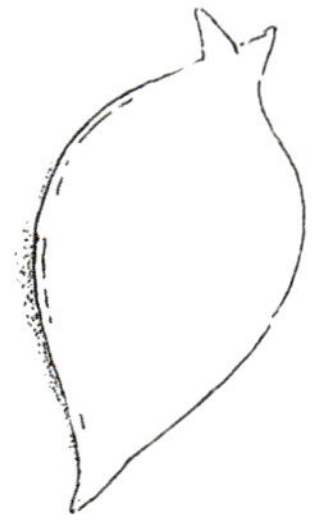

Lightly rub palms with vegetable oil to ensure that the dough doesn't stick. Take a small amount of dough in hand, roll it into a ball, and give it a conical shape. Use the index finger to make a cavity at the base of the dough by turning it constantly and add about 2 tablespoons of the filling. Then close the opening by slowly squeezing the filled dough with the index finger and thumb, and rotating it constantly, and give it a fishtail-like shape. Making a perfect *yomari* requires some practice. Follow the process as shown in the illustrations.

Steam the *yomari* for about 12–15 minutes, and they are ready.

I love the light bitterness of *chaku*, which balances the sweetness and nuttiness of the roasted sesame seeds, and can never get enough of this sweet fluffy delicacy.

JUJU DHAU

Bhaktapur's creamy yoghurt

There is a legend that a Malla king once organised a yoghurt competition in the Valley and Bhaktapur's yoghurt was found to be the best. Thereafter, it was known as *juju dhau*, literally the 'king of yoghurt' or 'king's yoghurt'. This extremely delicious, thick, creamy, sweet yoghurt has great significance in festivals and auspicious ceremonies in the Newa community. In fact, no *bhoye* is complete without it. *Juju dhau* is traditionally prepared by boiling buffalo milk together with spices like cardamom in a large cast-iron pot *(karai)* and then fermenting it in a clay pot *(katara)*. One can eat *juju dhau* on its own or with beaten rice.

1 ½ litres of milk, preferably whole milk of buffalo
3–4 cardamom
4–5 tablespoons of sugar
2–3 tablespoons yoghurt, for starting culture

Boil the milk together with the crushed cardamom and sugar in a pot for about 20 minutes or until the milk volume is reduced by about one-third.

Let the milk cool and pour it into a clay pot from a height of one foot to make it frothy. (The clay pot needs to be cleaned thoroughly by soaking it in clean water for a couple of hours.)

Add about 2–3 tablespoons of yoghurt from the previous batch as a culture. Cover the pot with another clay pot upside down and wrap with a few layers of jute bags. Leave it in a warm place to culture. In summer, this process will take 5–6 hours, whereas in winter, it might take a day.

SAMAY-BAJI

Newa auspicious platter, food of the deities

Also considered the 'food of the deities', *samay-baji* is an auspicious set of a variety of food eaten during festivals, religious ceremonies, and celebrations. It is believed to bring prosperity, good health, and good luck. The set generally includes *baji* (beaten rice), *chhoyla* (barbecued meat mixed with spices), *musya* (roasted black soybean), *palu-lava* (ginger-garlic), *wo* (black lentil pancake), *sanya* (smoked fish), *bodi wala* (black-eyed beans with spices), *tukuncha* (fried mustard greens), and *khen* (boiled egg). It is often served with alcoholic drinks made from fermented rice: *thwon* (undistilled) and *aila* (distilled liquor).

During Yenya or Indra Jatra, large heaps of *samay-baji* are offered to the gods and displayed in mounds outside temples or in the neighbourhood chowk, and later distributed to the community as an offering from the gods. It is believed that the tradition of *samay-baji* began with the advent of the festival in the 10th century. During the festival, children go around their neighbourhoods singing *'la chaku wyaka samaya-baji, wolo wolo pulu kisi'*, which literally means 'we want *samay baji* with a piece of meat, here comes the white elephant'. A white elephant is the carrier or vehicle of the Hindu god Indra, the king of heaven, and the mythical story of the festival revolves around Indra's capture by Kathmandu's inhabitants for stealing a flower that's only available on earth.

To create a *samay-baji* platter, place a handful of *baji* on a plate and add small portions of *chhoyla, musya, palu-lava, bodi wala, tukuncha* including small whole *sanya, khen*, and *wo* around the *baji*.

For recipes of each item:

Musya: Roast some black soybeans, and sprinkle salt and red chilli powder, and drizzle some roasted mustard oil.

Palu-lava: Cut ginger and garlic in small slices and sprinkle some salt and red chilli powder.

Sanya: Fry small smoked fish in vegetable oil until they become brown and crispy.

Bodi wala: Soak some black-eyed beans overnight. Boil them until cooked and drain the water. Add salt, cumin, coriander, and red chilli powder, and chopped fresh coriander leaves.
Heat roasted mustard oil in a small pan, fry fenugreek seeds and turmeric powder. Immediately pour it over boiled black-eyed beans and mix them together.

Khen: Hard boil an egg, and peel off the shell. Heat a teaspoon of vegetable oil in a small pan, and fry the boiled egg for a couple of minutes.

Tukuncha: Chop some greens such as mustard greens, broad mustard leaves, or fenugreek greens and stir-fry them in mustard oil with fenugreek seeds, turmeric powder, ginger, and garlic.

Chhoyla: See page 19 for the recipe.

Wo: See page 13 for the recipe.

Rai & Limbu Cuisines

INGENIOUS, INDIGENOUS FLAVOURS FROM THE EASTERN HILLS

When I was in Indonesia for a year in 2010–2011, I enjoyed eating Indonesian fermented soybean *tempe*. I also learned then that the Japanese have a tradition of fermenting soybean into *natto* and *miso*. But it was only when I came back to Nepal that I learned we too have a tradition of fermenting soybean. Unbeknown to many Nepalis, the Limbu and Rai communities (collectively known as the Kirats) of Nepal's eastern hills have a long tradition of making fermented soybean. Commonly known as *kinema*, this naturally fermented bean has a pungent aroma and atypical flavour. For the Limbus and Rais, *kinema* is a beloved delicacy that sharpens appetites. It was partly my discovery of *kinema* that prompted me to begin exploring Nepal's food culture, which eventually led me to write this book.

According to the Mundhum, the Kirat oral scripture, soybean was the first crop to be domesticated and cultivated by the Kirats. Fermented soybean, which originated within the Limbu community, is considered one of the oldest food cultures of eastern Nepal. From the Limbus, *kinema* made its way to other Kirat communities and spread further east. It is possible that the culture of fermenting soybean came to eastern Nepal from Yunnan, South China, by the 7th century, as one of the Limbu clans is believed to have their roots in Yunnan.

The Kirats have been living in the eastern Himalayan region for thousands of years. Kirat sub-groups differ in custom, language, and cuisine. As per the Mundhum, the Kirats became farmers from hunter-gatherers after their supreme god gave them the seeds of various crops: soybean, millet, rice, and sorghum. Millet is a particularly important crop, as it is a daily staple and also holds great cultural significance. *Dhindo*, a thick porridge-like dish, is prepared from millet flour and a staple meal of the Kirats. Alcohol made from millet is offered to ancestral deities, and required for every celebration and ritual. They offer *tongba*, an iconic alcoholic drink made from millet, to guests as a welcome gesture and sign of respect.

Limbu and Rai rituals and festivals are related to worshipping nature and ancestors. Chasok Tangnam and Sakela, the biggest festivals of the Limbus and Rais respectively, are observed by praying and thanking mother nature for a good harvest. They offer first harvested crops to the supreme god and ancestral deities. They also sacrifice a rooster and domesticated black pig *(sungur)* to ancestral deities during rituals and festivals.

Pork is the most celebrated meat in the community and is prepared into a wide variety of dishes, some of which are unique to the community. The meat is cooked with wild lichen *(yangben)* to make *yangben-phaksa.* Pig blood is mixed with *yangben* and minced meat including offal and fat, and encased in intestines to make blood sausage known as *sargemba. Yangben* is a cultural identity of the Limbu community. They always cook *yangben* with pork as it helps soak up the fat and lends a delicious earthy flavour. Pig fat is also preserved and used as cooking oil.

The Rais on the other hand have a special delicacy known as *wachipa,* where the burnt ash of a chicken's inner feathers is added to its meat and entrails, and cooked together. The burnt feathers add a peculiar flavour and a subtle bitterness to the dish.

Historically, beef was also consumed by the Kirats until cow slaughter was prohibited by the Hindu state of Nepal in the early 19th century.

The eastern hill communities also use many lesser-known wild spices in their cuisines. The use of these wild spices: *chimphing, khanukpa,* and *siltimmur* is largely limited to the region, where their distinctive flavours are used to flavour curries and achaars. Ginger, garlic, turmeric, chillies, and *timmur* are commonly used spices. *Dalle khursani* (cherry chilli) is a sought-after spice for its heat and flavour.

The cuisines of the Rais and Limbus are unlike any other, not just because they are deeply rooted in the environment, folk customs, and traditions, but also because they have largely remained intact, away from the influence of other cultures.

Chamre: Rice cooked slowly in mustard oil or ghee, turmeric powder, cumin seeds, fenugreek seeds, and salt.

Dhindo/Mangtak: Thick plain porridge-like made from millet or buckwheat flour, and sometimes with maize and wheat flour.

Chyankhlako Bhat: Cooked maize grits.

Kharen: Millet, maize, or wheat flour roti.

Sigolya/Pengoyla: Steamed barley or millet flour dough.

Papanda: Millet flour dough wrapped in leaves and roasted on an open fire.

Wachipa/Wamyuk/Wamrik/Tité: Special traditional dish prepared from cooking rice, minced rooster meat including offal with inner feather ash.

Selroti: Deep-fried ring-shaped *roti* made from rice flour batter and ghee.

Gormali: Sweet pudding made from milk and wheat flour dumplings, sometimes including rice; a common dish among the Sunuwar, one of the Kirat communities.

Kinema/Chembighik/Imbringgik: Fermented soybeans, usually cooked into a curry or soup.

Yangben phaksa: Pork curry with wild edible lichen and pig blood.

Sagi/Sigwa/Sasungi sumbak: Curry or thick soup prepared from tender leaves or tips and flowers of nettle greens.

Phando sumbak: Simple soup made from roasted soybean flour.

Phaksa-nudhi sumbak: Pork curry cooked with broad leaf mustard greens (*rayo saag*).

Sargemba/ Sargyangma: Blood sausage made from pig blood and minced pork, often with offal and wild lichen encased in a pig's intestines.

Lungghakcha: Unripe maize paste steamed by wrapping in its husk.

Gundruk: Fermented broadleaf mustard or radish greens

Chhop achaar: Dry powdered achaar prepared from oil seeds such as niger seeds (*philinge*), pumpkin seeds, with salt, spices, and concentrated lemon juice (*chuk*).

Singki: Fermented shredded radish.

Mesu/Phesuppa: Fermented bamboo shoot achaar.

Tongba: Alcoholic drink made from fermented millet served in a cylindrical-shaped vessel called *tongba*, with hot water.

Thi (jaand): Undistilled alcoholic drink prepared by fermenting millet grains, and sometimes from maize, wheat, etc.

Sijungwa (raksi): Distilled alcohol usually made from fermented millet.

CHAMRE

Turmeric and cumin rice

In Nepal's western hills where I grew up, *chamre* refers to a sweet rice dish prepared by cooking a local variety of aromatic or sticky rice (*anadi*) in ghee and sugar or sugarcane molasses. But in the eastern hills, *chamre* refers to a savoury dish prepared by cooking rice in mustard oil or ghee, turmeric powder, cumin seeds, fenugreek seeds, and salt. It is a common food eaten as a midday snack with some-kind of achaar. *Chamre* is slightly chewy and aromatic because of the spices and mustard oil or ghee. Turmeric gives it a bright yellow colour and adds flavour to the dish.

2 cups rice
1 teaspoon turmeric powder
1 teaspoon cumin seeds
1 teaspoon fenugreek seeds, optional
1 teaspoon salt
1 tablespoon minced ginger, optional
3–4 tablespoons mustard oil or ghee
Hot water

*Serves 4–5 people

Soak the rice for 15–20 minutes and drain the water.

Boil about 5–6 cups of water separately to cook the rice later.

Heat 3–4 tablespoons of ghee or mustard oil over medium heat in a pan. When the ghee or oil is hot, add the cumin and fenugreek seeds, minced ginger (optional), and turmeric powder. Add the soaked rice immediately and stir-fry for 3–4 minutes. Add some salt and pour in about a cup of hot water. Cook with the lid on until all the moisture is absorbed by the rice. Add more hot water, stir, and cook further with the lid on, and repeat the process another 3–4 times until the rice is cooked. It should take around 25–30 minutes until the *chamre* is ready to serve.

Chamre can be eaten with *philinge chhop*, *gundruk* achaar, or *kinema* achaar.

LUNGGHAKCHA

Steamed unripe maize paste wrapped in husk

Many people probably know about the traditional tamale from Mesoamerica, where maize was first domesticated by the indigenous people. A similar dish, *lungghakcha*, exists in the Limbu community, but unlike the tamale, it is prepared from unripe maize *(dudhilo/hariyo makai)*. I learned about this dish from the cookbook, *Limbu Khana ra Peyapadartha*, published by Kirat Yakthung Chumlung. Unripe maize is made into a paste, wrapped in its husk, and then steamed. Freshly harvested unripe maize is used as maize starts to lose its sweetness soon after the harvest. In the Limbu language, *lungghakcha* literally means round stone-shaped snack.

7–8 cobs of unripe maize

*serves 2–3 people

Remove a few layers of unblemished husk from fresh unripe maize carefully without any tears. They will be used as wraps later.

Remove all the remaining husk and hair-like silk from the maize. Then peel the kernels or cut them off the cob using a knife. Grind the kernels to make a fine paste. Traditionally, a stone grinder is used to make a paste. One can use an electric grinder for ease. Add a little water if required to maintain the consistency of the paste.

Take about 3–4 tablespoons of the paste and place it on the husk, making a rectangular shape. Layer with another husk and fold them, enclosing the paste completely, and tie with a strip of husk. Continue wrapping all the maize paste.

Then put them in a steamer and cook for about 12–15 minutes. The cooked *lungghakcha* is generally eaten with achaar. A simple achaar can be prepared by grinding green chillies, salt, and *timmur* together.

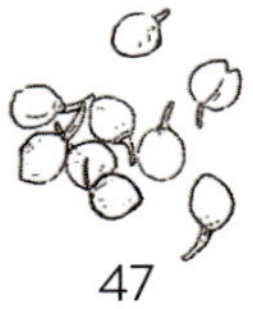

YANGBEN PHAKSA

Pork and wild edible lichen curry

This ethnic dish is one of the most popular delicacies of the Limbu community and nowadays, is also eaten by other Kirat communities. It is prepared by cooking *phaksa* (*sungur* or indigenous black pig meat), together with *yangben* (wild edible lichen), pig blood, and spices.

Yangben is the cultural culinary identity of the Limbus. The history of lichen consumption in Nepal probably has its origins in southern China's Yunnan region. Limbu ancestors came to Nepal's eastern hills from Yunnan via northern Burma and Assam, according to historians. According to the book *History and Culture of Kirat People*, by Imansingh Chemjong, the Limbus came to eastern Nepal around the 7th century and joined a related group, called Kirats, who came to the region much earlier. Lichen is considered ancient food in Yunnan. In Nepal, it's only the Limbus who have tradition of consuming lichen. Based on these information, it is plausible to surmise that the Limbus brought the practice of eating lichen from the Yunnan region.

To process lichen harvested from the forest, it is first boiled in water with firewood ash for several hours, then washed several times, and sun-dried to store. Alkaline ash removes the lichen's toxicity, reduces bitterness, and makes it tender. When cooked with pork meat and blood, it absorbs the fat and lends the meat an earthy flavour that is unique to the dish. It also helps in digestion and lowers the absorption of fat by the body from the pork.

1 kg pork meat, bone-in and skin-on with fat
A handful of *yangben*, pre-processed and dried
1 cup pig blood, preferably fresh
5–6 garlic cloves
A thumb-sized ginger
1 onion
1 teaspoon cumin seeds
1 teaspoon coriander seeds
2–3 fresh or dried red chillies
1–2 tablespoons of vegetable oil
Salt as per taste

*serves 4–5 people

Grind the garlic, ginger, cumin seeds, coriander seeds, and chillies together to make a paste.

Place the *yangben* in a large bowl and soak with a cup of hot water for about 5 minutes. Squeeze the water out of the *yangben*. Add the pig blood, half of the spice paste and a little salt, and then mix together. This mixture will be added to the pork curry later.

Heat about 1–2 tablespoons of vegetable oil in a wok or frying pan over medium heat. When the oil is hot enough, add the turmeric powder and chopped bone-in and skin-on pork with fat. Fry the meat for around 15 minutes, stirring frequently until some of the fat melts and the meat turns light brown.

Add the finely chopped onion, the remaining spice paste, and salt. Cook until the onion and spice paste turn light brown and the raw smell disappears.

Finally, add the *yangben*-blood-spice mixture. Cook for another 12–15 minutes with the lid on, stirring occasionally. The *yangben phaksa* can be eaten on its own, or with rice or *selroti*.

Note: *Yangben* isn't easily available. Outside the eastern hills, it is generally available in areas inhabited by the Rais and Limbus.

SARGEMBA

Pig blood sausage with wild lichen

Several Nepali ethnic communities, especially in the mountainous regions, make blood sausage, but the majority of the Nepali populace is unaware of this practice. The Sherpas and Tibetan descent communities make sausage from yak or sheep blood, which they call *gyurma*. In the Manang region, locals call it *khurung*. The Thakalis make sausage from mountain goat blood and call it *dhong* or *ghinti*. The Newas make sausage from buffalo blood and call it *jhuku*. Similarly, the Limbus make sausage from the blood of local black pigs; they call it *sargemba* or *sargyangma*. Generally, fresh blood is mixed with minced meat (including the internal organs), fat, and a few spices to make blood sausage. Intestines are used as casing. Some also add rice, roasted barley flour or buckwheat flour to the blood sausage.

Sargemba is a delicacy of the Limbu community, and often prepared during major festivals. It is prepared by mixing fresh pig blood, minced pork including the internal organs and fat, wild lichen and spices, and encased in intestines. *Sargemba* has a rich earthy flavour from the blood and lichen. The fat also enhances the flavour.

500–600 gm minced pork including fat
2 cups pig blood, preferably fresh
A handful of *yangben*
2 tablespoons garlic and ginger paste
40–50 cm long intestine, for encasing
1–2 tablespoons vegetable oil
Salt as per taste

Soak the *yangben* in hot water for about 5–10 minutes, and drain the water.

Place the minced pork, blood, and soaked *yangben* in a large bowl. Add the salt and ginger-garlic paste, and mix all the ingredients by hand. If the blood is clotted, break the clots by hand.

Clean the intestines in and out thoroughly with water.

Tie the one end of the intestine using a fiber and fill it with the mixture using a spoon or funnel, compacting regularly by hand. This process will probably need an extra set of hands. When done filling, tie the other end.

Boil or steam the *sargemba* for about 15–20 minutes on medium-low heat. Leave it to cool at room temperature. It can be stored in the refrigerator for later use.

Cut the *sargemba* into slices a few centimetres thick. Heat a pan and add 1–2 tablespoons of vegetable oil. Fry the *sargemba* on both sides for a couple of minutes. *The sargemba* can then be eaten hot with *timmur chhop* or tomato achaar.

PHAKSA-NUDHI SUMBAK

Pork curry with broad leaf mustard greens

Pork cooked with broadleaf mustard greens is very popular in the Kirat communities, as well as in other pork-eating ethnic communities of Nepal. Broadleaf mustard greens are the most commonly grown and consumed greens in Nepal. Pork and broadleaf mustard greens pair well together, and make for a delicious curry. Greens impart freshness to the curry and soak up all the fat and delicious flavour from the pork.

1 kg pork, bone-in skin-on with fat
A handful of broadleaf mustard greens
1 medium-sized onion
2–3 tomatoes
4–5 garlic cloves
1 thumb-sized ginger
1 teaspoon cumin seeds
1 teaspoon coriander seeds
2–3 red chillies
1 teaspoon turmeric powder
1–2 tablespoons vegetable oil
Salt as per taste

*serves 4–5 people

Heat 1–2 tablespoons of vegetable oil in a pan or *karai.*

Fry the finely chopped onion until soft and light brown, and then add turmeric. Immediately add bite-sized pieces of pork and cook over medium-high heat, stirring occasionally. Add salt halfway through cooking.

While the meat is cooking, make a spice paste out of the ginger, garlic, cumin seeds, coriander seeds, and red chillies using a mortar and pestle.

When the fat starts rendering and the meat turns a light brown, push the meat to one side of the pan and fry the spice paste in the rendered fat. Excess fat can be scooped out if preferred, and saved for cooking later. Add chopped tomatoes and mix them together. Cook for another 6–8 minutes with the lid on.

Wash the broadleaf mustard greens and cut them into one-inch-long pieces. Add them to the meat and give a good stir. Cook for another 6–8 minutes, stirring a couple of times. Do not overcook the greens so as to retain their freshness, crunchiness, and colour. Serve the *phaksa-nudhi sumbak* with rice, *dhindo,* or roti.

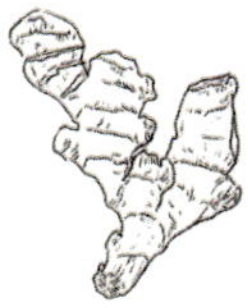

KINEMA

Fermented soybeans

Many may not be aware that Nepal has a culture of fermenting soybeans. The Rais and Limbus cook whole soybeans and let them naturally ferment for a couple of days. The fermented soybeans are known as *kinema*. The beans are then sun-dried for storage. The fermentation helps break the soy protein into easily digestible amino acids. *Kinema* has a pungent smell and a strong fermented flavour.

Packed with umami flavour, this fermented delicacy changed my perception of food: a dish that may not be appetising for some might be a cherished delicacy to others and that almost every taste is acquired and one has to train one's palate. It also inspired me to explore Nepal's diverse food culture and cuisine.

The word *kinema* is derived from the word *kinambaa* from the Limbu language, where *ki* means 'fermentation' and *nambaa* means 'flavour'. Depending upon the region and Kirat sub-groups, it is also known as *chembighik*, *imbringik*, and *hokuma*.

It is believed that the culture of making *kinema* originated in the Limbu community, which resides in the eastern Himalayan region: Terhathum, Taplejung, Panchthar, Dhankuta, and Ilam. There is no exact record of when and how the culture of fermenting soybeans was introduced to the eastern region of Nepal, but it is likely to be a more than 1,500-year-old tradition. Possibly, the culture of fermenting soybeans came from the Yunnan region of Southern China, which is believed to be the origin of non-salt based soybean fermentation. Also one of the Limbu clans came from the Yunnan region. The culture then spread to other communities and further east.

This nutritious ethnic food is traditionally prepared by wrapping boiled soybeans in banana leaves, wild ferns, or large ficus leaves, and left to ferment naturally for a day or a few days depending on the ambient temperature. These leaves not only help keep the soybeans warm and moist, but also contain microbes that help with the fermentation. *Bacillus subtilis* is the dominant microbe in natural fermentation, but other diverse types of bacteria, yeast, and microbes also play a role in imparting pungent and complex flavours. The wrapped soybeans are then put in a bamboo basket or jute bags, which help to keep them warm and provide a favourable environment for fermentation.

There is a slight variation in making the *kinema* among sub-groups and regions. Some lightly pound the boiled soybeans to break them into halves, some make a paste, and while others leave the soybeans whole for fermentation. The idea of breaking the soybeans is to increase the surface areas for microbial activity. Some dry the fermented soybeans under sunlight while others do it over a firewood oven.

The traditional indigenous knowledge or technique of making *kinema* has been passed down from one generation to the next. However, the present generation, especially living in urban areas, has rarely seen *kinema* being made and has almost forgotten the tradition.

Traditional process of making *kinema*

First, a local variety of dried brown soybeans are washed and soaked overnight in water.

The soaked soybeans are put into a large cooking pot. Enough water is added to fully submerge the soybeans and boiled for about an hour until cooked. Using a pressure cooker expedites the process.

Excess water is drained and the cooked soybeans are then lightly pounded in a large wooden mortar. This helps to speed up the fermentation process.

Some add firewood ash to maintain the alkaline state of *kinema*, which helps create a conducive environment for fermentation.

The soybeans are then placed in a bamboo basket lined with layers of locally found fresh fern fronds, banana leaves, or large ficus leaves, exposing the back surface. The powdery back surface of these leaves has microbes that help in the natural fermentation of *kinema* and the maintenance of the microbiota. Other wild leaves are also used to wrap the *kinema*.

The basket is then covered with jute bags and kept in the vicinity of a firewood oven to maintain the warm temperature favourable for fermentation, which takes 1–2 days in summer and 2–3 days in winter.

The fermented *kinema* has a slimy, viscous texture, and a slight odour of ammonia. The fermented beans can be consumed within 2–3 days in summer and within a week in winter without refrigeration. Genereally, the fermented beans are dried in the sun or over a firewood oven so that they remain edible for several months.

KINEMA SUMBAK

Fermented soybean soup or curry

My Rai and Limbu friends tell me that when they get a whiff of *kinema* being cooked, it whets their appetite. For others who did not grow up with *kinema*, its aroma might be too pungent, even offensive. The Rais and Limbus commonly cook *kinema* as a curry. This was also the first *kinema* dish I learned to cook. It is an acquired taste, but can be delicious and even addictive after one gets used to the smell. No wonder why it is a much-loved delicacy among the Limbu and Rai communities. *Kinema* is also used to make soups and achaars, and also to flavour daal and fried rice.

1 cup dried *kinema*
1 medium-sized onion, finely sliced
3–4 garlic cloves, minced
2–3 medium-sized tomatoes, finely chopped
2–3 green chillies, halved
1 teaspoon turmeric powder
2–3 tablespoons vegetable oil
A handful of fresh coriander leaves/garlic chives
Salt as per taste

*serves 3–4 people

Rinse the dried *kinema* to remove any impurities, and soak it in about two cups of hot water for about 10 minutes. Drain the water, but save it for later to make the soup.

In a pan, heat 2–3 tablespoons of vegetable oil over medium heat. Fry the finely sliced onions, halved green chillies, and minced garlic until they turn light brown. Add the turmeric powder and the *kinema* and fry for around 2–3 minutes. A pungent fermented aroma should start to release from the *kinema*. Add the finely chopped tomatoes and salt, and cook for another 3–4 minutes until the tomatoes melt. Add about 3–4 cups of water, including the water in which the *kinema* was soaked. Bring to a boil and cook for another 10–12 minutes over medium heat.

Garnish with the fresh coriander leaves or garlic chives and serve hot with steamed rice.

Note: To make *kinema* and *gundrukko jhol,* add a handful of soaked *gundruk* while frying the *kinema*.

KINEMA ACHAAR

Fermented soybean achaar

Dried *kinema* cooked with tomatoes makes for a very delicious achaar. It is also less pungent with the *kinema* acting more like a flavouring ingredient. The achaar can be stored for several days. Generally, dried *kinema* is used, but fresh fermented *kinema* can also be made into an achaar by mixing it with spices.

½ cup *kinema*
½ kg tomatoes, finely chopped
4–5 green chillies, halved
4–5 garlic cloves, finely sliced
1 teaspoon turmeric powder
1 teaspoon roasted *timmur*
1 teaspoon red chilli powder
3–4 tablespoons vegetable or mustard oil
Salt as per taste

Heat about 3–4 tablespoons of vegetable oil in a frying pan over medium heat. Fry the finely sliced garlic.

Add the *kinema* and fry it for about a minute or until an aroma develops. Then add turmeric powder and halved green chillies. Stir and add chopped tomatoes. Add the red chilli powder and salt to taste. Cook for around 8–10 minutes over medium heat with the lid on. Make sure to stir occasionally so that the bottom doesn't burn.

Once the tomatoes melt and form a thick gravy, remove the lid, reduce the heat to low, and cook for another 12–15 minutes, stirring occasionally until the moisture reduces and the oil starts to surface.

Sprinkle the roasted *timmur* grounds, add some lime or lemon juice, and give it a stir. Turn off the heat and let it cool. The achaar can be eaten as a relish with rice or roti. It can also be stored in a jar, topped with a tablespoon of vegetable oil to prevent mould. It will last for a week, and a couple of weeks if kept in a refrigerator.

SUNGURKO KHUTTAKO ACHAAR

Pork trotter achaar

The Rais and Limbus make use of all the pig's parts by cooking them into various delicacies. Nose-to-tail eating is ingrained in Nepali culture, and nothing is wasted. Pork trotters are slow-cooked with lots of spices and chillies to make a delicious spicy achaar.

1 kg pork trotters *(sungurko khutta)*
2 medium-sized onions
4–5 garlic cloves
1 thumb-sized ginger
3–4 tomatoes
4–5 fresh chillies
1 teaspoon fenugreek seeds
1 teaspoon cumin seeds
1 tablespoon cumin and coriander powder, optional
3–4 tablespoons red chilli powder
1 teaspoon turmeric powder
1–2 tablespoons mustard or any vegetable oil
1 lemon
Salt as per taste

*serves 4–5 people

Finely chop the onions, and make a garlic and ginger paste. Cut the chillies in half and chop tomatoes.

Heat 1–2 tablespoons of mustard oil in a large pan or pressure cooker over high heat. When the oil is hot enough, add the chopped pork trotters. Fry them for about 10–12 minutes, stirring occasionally, until light brown and the fat melts. Lower the heat and scoop out some of the melted fat, which can be used later for cooking.

Push aside the trotters, and fry the fenugreek and cumin seeds in the melted fat. Add the finely sliced onions, and then ginger and garlic paste, and fry until they turn light brown. Add the turmeric powder and mix together. Add the chopped tomatoes, salt, and red chilli, cumin, and coriander powder. Cook for about 5–6 minutes with an occasional stir until the tomatoes soften. Then add about two cups of water, put the lid on, turn down the heat to lowest, and cook for about 20 minutes or for 5–6 whistles. Shake the pressure cooker occasionally to check the moisture inside. If using a pan, add more water and cook for at least 40–45 minutes or until tender over low-medium heat.

When moisture is completely gone, take the lid off of the pressure cooker, squeeze some lemon juice, and cook for a few more minutes. The delicious spicy pork trotter is ready and can be eaten as a side dish with the main meal. It can also be stored for a few days.

PHILINGEKO CHHOP

Niger seed dry achaar

Niger seeds, known as *philinge* or *jhuse til* in Nepal, are used to make achaar by many hill communities. *Chhop* is dry achaar made from roasted oil seeds and spices. *Phlinge chhop* is popular among Rai and Limbu communities, eaten as a relish with a main dish as any other pickle or achaar to stimulate the taste buds and add flavour. Generally, *chuk* (concentrated large lemon or *nibuwa* juice) is added to give acidity to the *chhop*. *Chuk* is very sour and has a smoky flavour as it is concentrated by cooking over a firewood oven. This process helps preserve the lemon juice and can be used whenever fresh lemons are not available. Similar achaars can also be prepared from roasted soybeans, and pumpkin and sesame seeds. Often, *chimping* or Nepali hogweed (*Heracleum nepalense*) is added to the achaar to give it more flavour. This achaar can be stored for several weeks.

1 cup *philinge*
1 teaspoon of red chilli powder
1 teaspoon of *timmur*
1 teasoon *chimping*, optional
1 teaspoon of salt
½ teaspoon of *chuk*, or lemon juice

Roast the *philinge* and *timmur* lightly in a pan until they become aromatic. Transfer to a plate and let them cool.

Put the roasted *philinge* and *timmur* together with some salt, *chimping* (optional), and chilli powder in a mortar and pestle or electric grinder. Grind them together until they form a powder. Add the *chuk* (or fresh lemon juice), mix them together, and store in an airtight jar.

GORMALI

Sweet pudding with wheat flour dumplings

Gormali is a festive dish from the Sunuwar community, a Kirat sub-group. It is eaten during their biggest festival Folsyandar or Sakela. It is prepared from milk and wheat flour dough. Sometimes rice is also added. The recipe and ingredients are very similar to that of khir, but with wheat flour dumplings. The dumplings are usually prepared with flour made from freshly harvested wheat.

1½ litres milk
½ cup rice
½ cup whole wheat flour
4–5 tablespoons sugar
4–5 cardamom

*serves 3–4 people

Heat the milk in a cooking pot over medium heat. Add the sugar and crushed cardamom pods. While the milk is heating, make whole wheat flour dough and leave it covered.

After the milk starts boiling, add about a half cup of rice and cook for about 20–25 minutes over low-medium heat while stirring occasionally. Be careful not to burn the bottom of the pan while the quantity of the milk reduces by half and thickens.

Take a little bit of dough at a time in hand, make a small round ball, flatten it, and give it a concave-disc shape by pressing down with the thumb. The shape will hold the thickened pudding while eating. Add them to the pudding and cook for another 15 minutes, stirring occasionally. The *gormali* is ready.

JAAND RA TONGBA

Traditional fermented millet alcoholic drinks

Jaand and *Tongba* are traditional alcoholic beverages made by fermenting millet using locally-made yeast cake, known as *marcha* in Nepali. In the Rai and Limbu communities, alcoholic drinks, especially the iconic *tongba*, is central to any festival or celebration. It is offered to the gods and served to guests as a welcome drink. *Jaand*, also known as *chhyang*, is equally popular among other ethnic communities such as Magar, Gurung, Tharu, Tamang, Sherpa, Newa, etc.

Fermented millet grains are mixed with water, squeezed by hand and the liquid is filtered to extract a light coloured alcoholic drink, *jaand*. *Tongba* is brewed using hot water in a wooden, bamboo, or metallic cylindrical vessel known as *tongba*, after which the alcoholic drink is named, and imbibed using a bamboo or metal pipe perforated at its ends. For fermenting, *marcha* is added to cooked starchy millet grains and left to ferment for over a week to several months. *Marcha* is generally made from various wild herbs and plants containing yeast and cultured using millet flour. *Jaand* can also be made from other starchy grains such as rice, maize, wheat, barley, etc.

1 kg millet
4–5 tablespoons *marcha*

Fermenting

Wash the millet grains thoroughly to remove any impurities. Remove the grains that float.

Add the washed millet grains in a large pot, pour the water fully submerging the grains, and boil until cooked. Pinch a few grains with fingers to check if they are cooked. If the grains break easily, they are ready. Spread the cooked millet grains on a clean flat surface or tray to cool.

When they cool, break *marcha* by hand or using a mortar and pestle into a powder, and sprinkle over the cooked grains. A few tablespoons of *marcha* should be enough for a kilogram of millet grains. Mix them thoroughly using hands, and place in a clean sterile jar for fermentation. Do not make the jar airtight; cover it with a muslin cloth.

Keep the jar in a warm place. Fermentation takes about a week in summer and longer in winter. The longer the millet grains are fermented, the higher their alcoholic content.

Extracting or brewing

To extract *jaand*, place the fermented millet grains in a container and add water, about double in amount to the fermented millet grains. The quantity of water can vary according to how thick and strong one wants the *jaand* to be. Mash the mixture by hand for some time, squeeze and strain the liquid through a sieve to extract. If the *jaand* is too thick or strong, add some more water.

To make *tongba*, fill a *tongba* jar with the fermented millet grains and pour hot water over them. Leave for a couple of minutes to brew and then imbibe using a pipe made specifically for *tongba*. Refill the jar with hot water a couple of times for brewing.

Thakali Cuisine

HEARTY FLAVOURS FROM THE INNER HIMALAYAS

The Thakalis are renowned throughout Nepal for their wholesome, balanced, and delectable *thakali khana*: cooked rice or buckwheat *dhindo* (thick porridge-like dish) with black lentil or bean daal (soup), vegetable curry, meat curry, and achaar. *Thakali khana* has unique flavours from Himalayan ingredients and spices like *timmur, jimbu* (wild Himalayan allium), and *ghoini* (caraway seeds). *Timmur* is mainly used in making achaar while *jimbu* and *ghoini* are used to flavour daal and curry. Daal is the highlight of *thakali khana.* Lentils or beans are traditionally slow-cooked in a cast-iron pot and flavoured with garlic, *jimbu,* and ghee, giving the daal a rich flavour, thick consistency, and a greenish tint.

The Thakalis historically originated from the Thak Khola of Mustang in the rain shadow of the high Himalayas, but now are scattered throughout Nepal and abroad. Aside from their delicious *khana,* the Thakalis are also known for their clean and decorative kitchens, their hospitality, and trans-Himalayan trading occupation. From the 19th to the 20th centuries, many Thakali families held a monopoly over the trade route from the Gandak region to Tibet. Grains from Nepal and even goods from India were traded for Tibetan salt.

Buckwheat is the primary crop and is central to Thakali cuisine. Buckwheat flour is mostly made into *dhindo* and roti. The flour is also prepared into fries known as *kanchemba,* hand-torn noodle soup called *alangkhu,* and even blood sausage called *dhong* or *ghinti.* Buckwheat greens are sun-dried to preserve for the winter and dry seasons, which are ground to powder and cooked into soup known as *dhoprakhu.* As the high mountain climate doesn't support agriculture all year round, mountainous communities have a strong tradition of preserving produce.

The Thakalis also commonly consume barley, naked barley, millet, and maize. In early days, rice was reserved only for special occasions. They roast barley and naked-barley and grind into flour, and also ferment the grains to make alcoholic drinks.

In Mustang, the communities use a local variety of radish that lends a strong pungent and peppery flavour to their cuisine. They make the radish into delectable fresh achaar, and also add to soups and stews. They also preserve it by fermenting and sun-drying when abundant.

The Thakalis celebrate Toran La as the New Year, on the same day as the Hindu festival of Holi. The festival is an occasion to worship gods, pay homage to ancestors, and celebrate with family. There is plenty of good food, drinks, archery, and gambling. It is also considered an auspicious day for matchmaking. Mountain goats, sheep, or yaks are slaughtered during the festival. They prepare a variety of meat dishes including blood sausage and spicy sour goat head soup *(lepukhu)*. They also smoke-dry blood sausage and meat, including bone-in meat, over a firewood oven for preservation. The preserved meat can be stored for several months and later cooked with vegetables to make curry and stew. The Thakalis adore the smoke-dried meat of the mountain goat.

As the Thakalis reside in the intermediary zones between the lower hills and the higher Himalayas, and also because of the trans-Himalayan salt trade, their food culture is influenced by both lowland and highland cuisines. Rice and black lentils came from the lowlands whereas salty butter tea and roasted barley flour came from the trans-Himalayan region. Most Nepalis will know *Thakali khana*, but Thakali cuisine is far more interesting and has a wide variety to offer.

Ghoken (phaparko roti): Buckwheat flour roti.

Sangdhen (dhindo): Thick porridge-like dish made from buckwheat or millet flour.

Kalo maas/Mustang simiko daal: Thick soup prepared from black lentils or local beans, seasoned with ghee and *jimbu*.

Thakali khana: Thakali main meal, often consisting of buckwheat *dhindo* instead of rice, and daal made from either black lentils or local beans.

Alangkhu: Hand-torn buckwheat flour dumpling/noodle soup with smoke-dried meat, fresh greens, and radish.

Rasya (bhutuwa): Mountain goat, sheep or yak offal fried with spices.

Tyasyakhu: Soup made from a mountain goat's head and legs, and a few key spices like *timmur,* chilli, garlic, and salt.

Lepukhu: Spicy and sour soup made from a mountain goat head, including brain.

Pharokhu: Soup prepared from roasted white bean flour.

Dhoprakhu: Traditional soup prepared from dried buckwheat greens powder.

Kaprakhu: Barley soup.

Dhong/Ghinti: Thakali blood sausage made from sheep, mountain goat, or yak blood and offal, and sometimes with buckwheat flour.

Taya (aalu) dameko: Halved potato fried slowly in ghee on a pan over low heat.

Sukuti: Smoke-dried mountain goat, sheep, or yak meat.

Kanchemba: Crispy buckwheat fries, usually served with garlic-chilli achaar or *timmurko chhop.*

Taya (aalu) sukuti pla: Curry made from potato and smoke-dried meat flavoured with ghee and *jimbu.*

Timmurko chhop: Dry spice mixture of *timmur*, red chilli, and Himalayan rock salt.

Thepe: *Achaar* made from smashed radish with spices and *timmur.*

Phopke: Fermented rice dessert with ghee and sugar.

Jhaikhatte: Distilled barley or naked barley alcohol with rice grain tempered in ghee.

GHOKEN (PHAPARKO ROTI)

Buckwheat pancake or roti

Buckwheat is the traditional staple of the Thakali community. A highly adaptive crop that grows easily in low-fertility soil, buckwheat is cultivated in Nepal's highlands as well as lowlands. Two varieties of buckwheat are grown and consumed: *mithe phapar* (common buckwheat) and *tite phapar* (tartary buckwheat). Buckwheat flour is used to make a variety of dishes and is largely consumed as roti and *dhindo*. In the upper mountainous area of the far west, bitter buckwheat flour batter for making roti is prepared in a large wooden bowl made of birch or walnut wood, which is believed to reduce the bitterness and make the roti delicious.

Ghoken is prepared simply by cooking a batter made from buckwheat flour and water in a cast iron pan. It is eaten at any time of the day, as a breakfast or a main meal or a midday snack. It can be eaten simply with tea, or with daal, curry, and achaar.

2 cups buckwheat flour
2 cups water
2–3 tablespoons ghee or vegetable oil

*serves 3–4 people

Take the buckwheat flour in a large bowl. Add about two cups of water. Beat the mixture to make a thick batter and leave it to rest for about 5–10 minutes.

Heat a pan over medium heat and grease it lightly with the vegetable oil or ghee. When the pan is hot enough, add a ladle of batter. Spread it with the ladle or by hand giving a round shape and an even thickness. One may cook with the lid on. When the top layer of the pancake changes colour and becomes firm, flip it over. It takes about 2–3 minutes for each side to cook. Continue with the rest of the batter and stir the batter occasionally to ensure an even consistency.

The roti can be eaten with daal, curry, and/or achaar. Or one can simply drizzle some honey over the warm roti and have it for breakfast.

SANGDHEN (DHINDO)

Thick porridge of buckwheat or millet flour

Sangdhen (dhindo) is a thick porridge-like dish prepared by cooking buckwheat or millet flour in boiling water while stirring continuously. Many communities in the hilly and mountainous regions have a practice of eating *dhindo*, traditionally a main staple dish until rice became common. It is eaten with a variety of side dishes such as daal, curry, and achaar. While it is still perceived as a poor people's food, today, many Nepali restaurants serve the dish, as more people consider *dhindo* to be healthy.

2 cups buckwheat flour
2 cups water
2 tablespoons ghee, optional

*serves 3–4 people

Heat about two cups of water in a cooking pot or *kasaundi*, and sprinkle about a tablespoon of buckwheat flour. Adding a little flour beforehand helps reduce the formation of lumps later.

When the water starts boiling, gradually add the buckwheat flour and stir continuously with a wooden spatula. Soon it will start to thicken. When all the flour is added, lower the heat, grab the handle of the pot firmly with one hand, and stir continuously for about 10–12 minutes. Continue to stir in a folding and pulling pattern until all the lumps are gone and *dhindo* becomes thick and smooth. Making *dhindo* requires a fair amount of labour.

Serve a generous portion of the *dhindo* hot with curry, daal, and achaar. Pour some melted ghee over the *dhindo* to add flavour.

KANCHEMBA
Buckwheat fries

Kanchemba is a typical Thakali snack made from buckwheat flour and served with spicy *timmur*-tomato achaar or *timmur chhop*. First, buckwheat flour is cooked into *dhindo*, then rolled into small fingers and deep-fried. Frying in ghee imparts an aromatic buttery flavour and a crispy texture. *Kanchemba* is both nutritious and delicious.

1 cup buckwheat flour
1 cup water
2 cups ghee or vegetable oil, for frying
2 tablespoons *timmur chhop*, for dipping
Salt as per taste

*serves 3–4 people

First make *dhindo* by cooking the buckwheat flour in boiling water as described in the preceding recipe.

Let it cool for a couple of minutes, so that it can be comfortably molded by hand.

Rub some vegetable oil on your hands. Take a small marble-size portion of *dhindo*, give it a spherical shape first, and then make a small finger with tapered ends by rolling in between the palms. Repeat the process to make more fingers. This has to be done quickly or the *dhindo* will become firm when it cools.

In a frying pan, heat ghee or vegetable oil over medium heat. When the ghee or oil is hot enough, fry the buckwheat fingers for about 5–6 minutes. Fry them in small batches to make sure that they are light brown and crispy. Serve hot with *timmur chhop*.

THAKALI DAAL

Black lentil or local bean soup

Daal (lentil or bean soup) is the highlight of the Thakali *khana* set. Its rich flavour, creamy texture, peculiar greenish colour, and distinctive aroma come from the ingredients used and the cooking process. Black lentils grown in the lower hills and beans grown locally at high altitudes are used to make Thakali daal. Traditionally, they are slow cooked in a cast iron pot over firewood and seasoned with ghee and *jimbu*, the most essential flavouring ingredients in Thakali cuisine. Slow-cooking makes the daal extra creamy while the ghee and *jimbu* add aroma and flavour, and cooking in a cast iron pot imparts a peculiar greenish colour.

1 cup black lentils or local beans, split
2–3 garlic cloves
½ thumb-sized ginger
½ teaspoon turmeric powder
Salt as per taste

Tempering spices
2 tablespoons ghee
1–2 garlic cloves
1–2 dry red chillies
1 tablespoon cumin and coriander powder mix
1 teaspoon turmeric powder
1 tablespoon *jimbu*

*serves 3–4 people

Wash a cup of black lentils or split local beans and put them in a pressure cooker with about 3–4 cups of water. Add the smashed ginger and garlic cloves, salt, and a pinch of turmeric powder. Put the lid on and cook over low heat for around 25–30 minutes or for about 7–8 whistles. Check the water content occasionally by shaking the cooker to make sure the daal doesn't get burnt. Turn off the heat and leave it to rest. Do not force the steam out of the pressure cooker.

Open the lid after the steam is all gone and transfer the beans into a cast-iron pot. Lightly mash with a spatula to thicken the daal. Add about 3–4 cups of hot water and cook over medium heat for around 12–15 minutes. Taste and adjust the salt if necessary.

To temper the spices, heat about two tablespoons of ghee in a cast-iron saucepan over medium-low heat. When the ghee is hot, add the cumin seeds, dry red chillies, finely chopped garlic, and *jimbu*. Turn off the heat and add the turmeric powder. Pour it immediately over the daal. It will make a sizzling sound. The tempering of spices imparts an aromatic, garlicky, buttery, and smoky flavour to the dish.

GHINTI DHOPRAKHU

Thakali blood sausage and buckwheat greens flour soup

When young buckwheat greens are a plenty in season, they are sun-dried, ground, and stored for the winter and dry seasons when greens are not as easily available. Known as *dhopra,* this traditional survival food is slowly disappearing. In the Thakali language, *dho* means 'greens', *prah* means 'flour', and *khu* usually refers to 'soup, daal or stew'. The Thakalis make soup from *dhopra*, which is eaten as an alternative to daal. People from Manang also consume it and they call it *pote.*

The Thakalis make blood sausage, known as *ghinti* or *dhong*, similar to *gyurmc* that the Sherpas and Tibetans make. Blood and offal of sheep, mountain goat, or sometimes yak are encased in intestines to make *ghinti.* The Thakalis also make *ghinti* from blood and buckwheat flour. It is either consumed directly after boiling or smoke-dried for later. The first time I had blood sausage was about a decade ago at a small eatery in Kagbeni, Mustang. Until then, I didn't know that the practice of making blood sausage existed in Nepal. The blood sausage was hung over a firewood oven for smoke-drying, and simply fried before serving. I still remember its flavour. Served with naked-barley alcohol, it tasted delicious with *timmur chhop.*

Dhopra, when cooked with *ghinti* or alternatively with smoke-dried meat, acquires a smoky meaty flavour and makes the soup delectable.

200 gm smoke-dried *ghinti*
3–4 tablespoons *dhopra*
5–6 garlic cloves
1 thumb-sized ginger
1–2 fresh or dried chillies
1 teaspoon turmeric powder
1 teaspoon *ghoini* (caraway seeds), optional
2–3 tablespoons vegetable oil
Salt as per taste
1 lemon

*serves 3–4 people

Soak the *ghinti* in hot water for 10–15 minutes and cut into bite-sized pieces. Soaking in hot water makes the ghinti tender and easier to cook.

Grind the garlic, ginger, *ghoini*, and red chillies in a mortar and pestle to make a fine paste.

Heat a pot over medium heat and add 2–3 tablespoons of ghee or vegetable oil. When the oil is hot enough, add the *ghinti* and fry for a couple of minutes. Push it to a side of the pot, and add the spice paste and turmeric powder. Fry them for a minute, until the raw smell goes away.

Add 4–5 cups of water and then salt. Bring to a boil and then add 4–5 tablespoons of *dhopra,* which thickens the soup. Cook for another 12–15 minutes and the *ghinti dhoprakhu* is ready.

Serve it hot in a bowl together with some lemon slices. Squeeze some lemon juice into the soup to balance the taste of the *dhopra.* It can be eaten with buckwheat roti, *dhindo,* rice, or simply as a soup.

Sonam Dorjee Gurung

ALANGKHU

Buckwheat flour dumpling soup with smoke-dried meat and vegetables

Alangkhu is a hand-torn or hand-rolled buckwheat flour dumpling or noodle soup with smoke-dried mountain goat meat and vegetables. Smoke-dried meat, *sukuti,* is a traditional delicacy. Making *sukuti* is a common way to preserve proteins in mountainous regions where crops can't be grown all year round.

Smoked-dried bone-in meat is added to *alangkhu* to give it a rich, meaty, smoky flavour. The dish is similar to the Sherpa *shyakpa* or *thenthuk,* but with buckwheat flour noodles or dumplings instead of wheat flour.

1 cup buckwheat flour, to make dumplings or noodles
150–200 gm smoke-dried meat
1 small radish
1 small carrot
3–4 stalks broadleaf mustard greens *(rayo saag),* optional
4–5 garlic cloves
½ teaspoon turmeric powder
1 teaspoon red-chilli powder
1 teaspoon *timmur*
1 tablespoon vegetable oil
1–2 tablespoons *timmurko chhop,* as condiments
Salt as per taste

*serves 3–4 people

First prepare buckwheat flour dough to make dumplings or noodles. Take about a cup of buckwheat flour in a bowl and pour about a quarter cup of water, mixing them slowly. Knead the dough for a few minutes. Cover the dough and let it rest for 10–15 minutes.

In a cooking pot, add bite-sized pieces of smoke-dried meat and pour about 4–5 cups of water. Turn on the heat and bring the water to a boil. Smash the garlic cloves and add to the pot. Pour a tablespoon of vegetable oil. Add the turmeric and red chilli powder, coarse *timmur* grounds, a tablespoon of buckwheat flour, and some salt. Boil for about 15–20 minutes until the meat becomes tender.

While the soup is boiling, add thin slices of the radish and carrot. Then take the buckwheat flour dough, stretch it, and make small finger-shaped dumplings with tapered ends or hand-torn noodles of a preferred shape and size, and add them into the soup. Boil for another 12–15 minutes or until cooked. Chop the greens and add to the soup. Cook for another 3–4 minutes and the soup is ready. Serve this simple nutritious soup with *timmur chhop* as a condiment, which makes the soup more flavoursome.

LEPUKHU

Spicy sour goat head soup

Every part of an animal is made into some kind of delicacy. The Thakalis make a spicy, tangy thick soup or stew from goat head meat, including the brain, known as *lepukhu*. It is mainly prepared during the *Toran la* festival. Every part of goat head has a different taste and texture, which makes the soup more interesting. The brain is mashed up into the soup, which gives it a thick gooey texture.

500–600 gm goat head meat, including brain
1 medium-sized onion
5–6 garlic cloves
1 thumb-sized ginger
1 teaspoon turmeric powder
1 teaspoon cumin powder
1 tablespoon red chilli powder
1 teaspoon *timmur*
2–3 tablespoons vegetable oil
1 teaspoon *chuk* (evaporated Nepali lemon juice) or 2–3 tablespoons lemon juice
A handful of fresh coriander leaves
Salt as per taste

Remove the bones from goat head and cut out the head meat, including the tongue, but excluding the brain into small bite-sized pieces.

In a cooking pot or pressure cooker, heat about 2–3 tablespoons of vegetable oil. Finely slice the onion, make a ginger and garlic paste, and add them into the pot.

Fry them until they turn light brown. Then add the turmeric powder. Immediately add the goat head meat and fry for 10–12 minutes, stirring occasionally. Then add the salt, cumin powder, red chilli powder, and *timmur* grounds. Cook for another 4–5 minutes, stirring occasionally.

Add about 3–4 cups of hot water into the pot. When the water starts boiling, mash up the brain by hand and add to the soup. Cook over slow heat for about 20–25 minutes in a pot or for 3–4 whistles in a pressure cooker. When the meat is well cooked, add *chuk* or some lemon juice, and cook for another couple of minutes. Garnish with the fresh coriander leaves.

TIMMUR CHHOP

Nepali pepper spice mix

Timmur chhop is a typical Thakali spice-mix. It is used as a dry condiment in the soups or to dip boiled or fried potatoes, *kanchemba*, and fried *ghinti* (sausage). It is prepared with just three ingredients: *timmur*, dry red chillies and salt. *Timmur* is similar to the Sichuan pepper, but has a slightly different flavour profile with citrusy notes and a less numbing quality.

3–4 tablespoons *timmur*
100 gm dry red chillies
2 tablespoons Himalayan white rock salt, or common salt

Lightly roast the *timmur* in a pan and let it cool.

Place all the three ingredients in a mortar and pestle or an electric grinder, and grind them. To make the *chhop* that's less spicy, use larger deseeded chillies.

Chhop can be made in a large batch and can be stored for several months in a jar.

THEPE ACHAAR

Freshly smashed radish achaar

Radish achaar, either fermented or fresh, is a common Thakali relish. Fresh radish is smashed on a traditional flat stone mortar and pestle *(silauto)* and mixed with spices to make *thepe* achaar. The word *thepe* means smashed in the Nepali language. The achaar has a fresh crunchy texture, a peppery flavour from the radish, and a numbing-tingling-citrusy flavour from the *timmur*.

Many hill communities also make this achaar. Whenever radish was in season, my mother would make *thepe* every so often. It is very easy and quick to make, and is usually eaten as a relish with *daal-bhat-tarkari* or roti.

1 medium-sized radish
1–2 fresh green chillies, optional
1 tablespoon *timmur chhop*
A handful of fresh coriander leaves, for garnishing

Clean the radish properly and cut it into small finger-sized pieces. Do not remove the skin, as it has an intense spicy and pungent flavour that adds to the taste of the achaar.

Place some radish pieces, green chillies, and about a tablespoon of *timmur chhop* in a mortar and pestle, and smash or pound them to form a kind of minced or shredded radish. Add more radish pieces and continue smashing them. Mix them well together and the fresh *thepe* achaar is ready. Garnish with the fresh coriander leaves.

Tharu & Maithili Cuisines

TASTE OF THE ALLUVIAL SOUTHERN PLAINS

The plains of Southern Nepal, known as the Tarai or Madhes, are fertile alluvial deposits, making the region a primary producer of grains in the country. Both large and small rivers are in abundance in the Tarai, which help in agriculture and also make fish a big part of the regional diet. The region is also a confluence of different cultures and religions, and its food culture, in general, is shaped by the alluvial flooded plains, fresh water bodies, and dense forests.

The Tharus and Maithils are the indigenous inhabitants of the southern plains. The Maithil community resides between the Gandaki and Koshi rivers in eastern Nepal, and also in the adjoining Indian region spreading up to the Ganga river. The Maithils share their cuisine on both sides of the border. The Tharus meanwhile largely inhabit the inner plains across the length of Nepal. They have considerable regional diversity in their cuisines. Eastern Tharu cuisine has some similarities with Maithili cuisine because of the geographical and cultural contiguity.

The Tharus are by large foragers, fishers, and subsistence farmers. Grown abundantly in the southern plains, rice is an essential part of their cuisine. In particular, *andik,* the only variety of sticky rice grown in Nepal, is a cultural food and consumed during festivals and celebrations. Even though priority is now given to commercial rice varieties, Tharu families continue to allocate small plots of land for *andik* cultivation. *Andik* rice is soaked and steamed to make *chichar;* it is also fermented to make the alcoholic drink *andik jaar*; and *andik* flour is made into deep-fried roti.

As the Tharus live close to rivers and fresh water bodies, fishing is a way of life. *Ghonghi,* which are freshwater snails, are collected from small rivers, ponds, canals or irrigated paddy fields. The snails are cleaned and made into a curry with traditional spices, a much-loved delicacy in the community.

Maghi is their new year and biggest festival, which is observed by cleaning and decorating houses, doing puja, performing the *sakhiya* dance, and making festive food items. The Western Tharus make *dhikri* (a steamed rice flour dumpling) and the eastern Tharus make *bagiya* (a flattened steamed rice flour dumpling often filled with mashed lentils or potatoes). Maghi celebration also usually involves *andik* roti, *chichar,* tuber vegetables, laddu (sesame-jaggery balls), *ghonghi,* fish, and meat dishes. Pigs are slaughtered a day

before the festival in a customary practice known as *jita-marne*, which is more prevalent in the west. Pigeon meat is common in the east and duck meat in the central region. Tharu as well as a few other communities in the southern plains also consume rodents found in the paddy fields as a delicacy. A large variety of legumes and beans such as black lentils, horse gram, *khesari,* and red lentils form a large and important part of their food culture.

Historically a kingdom, Mithila's rich agrarian civilisation dates back to the late Vedic period (1100–500 BCE). The alluvial plains of the region and irrigation helped agriculture flourish since ancient times. Rice and wheat, the primary staples of this area, are cropped alternatively in the growing season: rice in monsoon and wheat in winter.

Freshwater fishes are important part of Maithili cuisine too. No celebration or function is complete without fish. *Machh-bhat* or fish curry with rice is a perennial favourite.The Maithils cook fish in mustard oil and with a mustard seed paste. Mustard seeds are used extensively in cooking, mainly as a flavouring ingredient. Mustard oil is an essential cooking medium, also used across Nepal as traditional cooking oil. Sesame seeds are also used in the Maithil kitchen and in religious rituals as they are considered holy.

Another common festive Maithili food is *kadhi-badi,* which is prepared by cooking gram flour dumplings in a yoghurt-based soup. *Taruwa* is a special delicacy prepared by deep-frying vegetables in gram flour or rice flour batter. *Kadhi-badi* and *taruwa* are often prepared for esteemed guests. *Khichadi*—rice cooked with lentils and spices together—is a weekly affair in the Maithil community unlike in the Khas-Pahadi community where it is prepared only a couple of times a year during festivals.

Cow's milk and dairy products such as ghee, yoghurt, and *khuwa* (evaporated milk solids) are central to Maithili food culture. These food items are categorised as *shuddha* or pure, a concept derived from Hindu food practices, and are thus used for religious purposes too. Maithil food is, in fact, largely guided by Hindu cultural practices and rituals.

The Maithils also make a variety of sweets and confection using milk, dairy products, and jaggery or sugar. The sweet culture in Maithili cuisine can be attributed to the cultivation of sugarcane, which is an important historical crop in the region. Sugarcane juice is boiled down to solids to make jaggery, which can then be stored for months. Khir (sweet rice or lotus seed pudding), *puwa* (rice flour cooked in ghee and sugar), halwa (semolina flour dessert), *malpuwa* (sweet deep-fried roti), and *gujiya* (sweet pastry stuffed with *khuwa*) are some of the sweet dishes prepared during religious ceremonies and festivals such as Holi. *Thekuwa*, a deep-fried cookie made from wheat flour, milk, and jaggery, is prepared during the Chhat festival, the biggest religious festival of the Maithils dedicated to the worship of the sun god.

Tharu and Maithil foods represent the diversity of food culture in the southern plains, which have evolved for hundreds of years.

Dhikri: Steamed rice flour dough, a festive delicacy of the Tharus living in the western plains.

Bagiya: Similar to *dhikri* but diamond shaped and often with a filling of cooked legumes, or potatoes mixed with spices, a festive delicacy of the Tharu and Maithil communities in the eastern plains.

Bhakka: Fluffy steamed rice flour cake, a popular dish of the *Rajbansi* community in the eastern region.

Chichar: Steamed *anadi* rice, a traditional variety of sticky rice grown in the western region.

Poka: *Chichar* wrapped in a leaf and roasted over embers or hot ash.

Ghonghi: Freshwater snail curry, popular among both the Tharu and Maithil communities.

Pakuwa: Dry-cooked meat of pork, wild boar, pigeon, or chicken with spices.

Katnausi: Meat of a pig, wild boar, or goat meat cooked together with its blood and spices.

Gengta/Kakhor/Kekhada: Small freshwater crabs cooked or fried together with spices.

Jhingiya machhari: Freshwater shrimp stir-fried together with spices.

Sipi/Situwa/Sutahi: Freshwater mussels, which are boiled first, their shells removed and cooked as a curry.

Patushni/Arikanchan/Khariya: A dish prepared from layers of taro leaves pasted with rice flour or legumes paste.

Sidharaa: Sun-dried ground taro stems and small dried fish cake or patties, cooked as a curry or soup.

Biriya: Withered greens mixed with rice or legume paste and spices, made into long nuggets, sun-dried, and eaten deep fried or as a curry.

Bayarak chutney: Spicy, sweet, and sour chutney made from *bayar* (wild Indian plum).

Sidhrak chutney: Chutney made from small dried fish and spices.

Tilauri (Tilke laddu): Small round-shaped festive sweets made from sesame seeds and jaggery.

Teli paur roti: Deep-fried roti made from rice flour batter, an essential food item during marriage ceremonies.

Aandik jhor/Jaar: Traditional alcoholic beverages made from a sticky rice variety known as *andik* or *anadi.*

Mahuwa: Liquor made from wild flowers called *mahuwa*.

Khichari: Commonly eaten delicacy prepared by cooking rice and lentils together with ghee and spices.

Choka/Bharta: Mashed roasted or boiled potatoes, brinjals, elephant foot yams with spices.

Chana daal puri: Pan-fried puri (roti) stuffed with cooked split gram and spices.

Machhka jhor: Fish curry usually cooked with mustard seed paste and spices. Rohu fish, a carp variety, is the most popular.

Kadhi-badi: Deep-fried gram flour dumplings and yoghurt curry or soup.

Adaurike tarkari: Sun-dried legume nugget curry.

Taruwa: Deep-fried potatoes and vegetables dipped in gram or rice flour batter.

Aalu bhujiya: Thinly-cut potatoes pan-fried to crisp.

Gujiya: Deep-fried sweet pastry filled with *khuwa*.

Thekuwa: Traditional sweet deep-fried cookies prepared with whole wheat flour, jaggery, milk, and ghee.

DHIKRI

Steamed rice flour dumpling

Dhikri, a simple dish prepared by steaming rice flour dough, is a cultural food of the Tharu community in the western plains. It is an essential food prepared during the Tharus' biggest festival, Maghi, which is also the beginning of the new year for the community. It can be made into different shapes representing the everyday tools and materials their livelihoods depend on, and is named accordingly. An elongated *dhikri* is the most common shape, called *lathha* or *sojuwa.* It is eaten with a curry, lentil soup, and/or achaar.

2 cups rice
About a cup of warm water

*Serves 3–4 people

Dhikri is usually prepared from freshly milled rice flour, as it tastes better. To make the flour, soak two cups of rice in water for 4–5 hours or overnight. Drain the water and grind the soaked rice into fine flour. Sift the flour to remove coarser particles if necessary. Traditionally, a *dhiki* or a *janto* was used to grind the flour.

Put the flour in a large bowl and pour in about a cup of warm water. Mix and knead the dough. Cover with a moist cloth for 10–15 minutes.

Take a small ball of dough and give it an elongated, cylindrical shape with slightly bulging ends using the palms. One can give it a variety of shapes.

Place the shaped dough in a steamer and steam for around 10–12 minutes. A momo steamer or simply a pot wrapped in a muslin or cotton cloth covered by a lid can be used for steaming. Traditionally, *dhikri* is steamed in a claypot or a *dhakiya,* a woven grass basket, over a boiling pot of water. Serve the *dhikri* hot with a curry, lentil soup, and/or achaar.

BAGIYA

Steamed rice flour dumplings, with lentil or potato filling

Whereas *dhikri* is a delicacy of the Tharu community living in the western plains, *bagiya* is a delicacy of the Tharus and Maithils living in the eastern plains. *Bagiya* is very similar to *dhikri*, but unlike *dhikri*, the rice flour dough is sometimes filled with cooked legumes, potatoes, and other vegetables fillings. Sometimes, rice flour is roasted before making the dough for *bagiya*. Like *dhikri*, *bagiya* is an essential dish during Maghi, the new year, and Shukrati, the festival of lights.

Dough
2 cups rice
About a cup of warm water

Filling
4 medium-sized potatoes, or 1 cup of split chickpeas
1 medium-sized onion
1 teaspoon garlic paste
1 teaspoon ginger paste
½ teaspoon cumin powder
½ teaspoon coriander powder
½ teaspoon turmeric powder
2–3 green chillies or ½ teaspoon chilli powder
2–3 tablespoons mustard or any vegetable oil
Salt as per taste

*Serves 3–4 people

To make the rice flour dough, soak two cups of rice in water for 4–5 hours or overnight. Drain the rice and grind into fine flour. If necessary, sift the flour to remove coarser particles. One can also use already milled rice flour. Add warm water to the rice flour, mix together, and knead the dough. Leave it covered (or it will dry and crumble) for at least 10–15 minutes.

To make the filling, boil potatoes or split chickpeas until they're well cooked. One can use a pressure cooker to speed up the process.

In a pan, heat 1–2 tablespoons of vegetable oil. Fry the garlic and ginger paste, and then add the finely chopped onion. Add the turmeric, cumin and coriander powder, and green chillies. Immediately add the cooked chickpeas or potatoes. Add some salt and mash the mixture with a spatula to make a paste. Make sure the spices are mixed properly. Cook for another couple of minutes.

To make *bagiya* without filling, take a small amount of dough and form a ball, and then give it a shape with tapered ends. Flatten it using the palm and fingers giving it a diamond-shaped.

To make *bagiya* with filling, take a small ball of dough, mold it into a small bowl shape, and add a tablespoon of the potatoes or chickpeas mixture to the middle. Enclose it carefully by first forming a ball and then giving it a shape with tapered ends. Flatten it using the palm and fingers so that it becomes diamond-shaped.

Steam the *bagiya* for around 12–15 minutes. Serve hot with a curry, lentil soup, and/or achaar.

CHICHAR

Steamed sticky rice

Like in many Southeast Asian countries, Nepal too has a culture of eating sticky rice, although it is generally eaten as a festive dish than a staple fare. *Chichar* is a popular Tharu dish prepared from steaming *anadi* rice, a sticky rice variety. The water drained after soaking *anadi* rice is believed to cure stomach ache and heatstroke. Traditionally, *chichar* is steamed in a basket made from bamboo or grass, or a porous clay pot. One can make it in a regular steamer that is used to make momos. This cooked *anadi* rice can be wrapped in leaves and roasted directly on a fire pit to make the other festive delicacy known as *poka*.

2 cups *anadi* rice

*Serves 3–4 people

Soak *the anadi* rice in water for at least 2–3 hours and drain.

Lay a piece of clean muslin cloth in a steamer and put the soaked rice over the cloth. Steam for about 20–25 minutes with the lid on. Serve it hot with a curry and achaar. In the central region, the Tharus prefer to eat *chichar* with duck meat curry.

To make *poka*, wrap the *chichar* with a few layers of banana or fig leaves, giving it a round shape, and roast on a fire pit for about 15–20 minutes.

GHONGHI

Freshwater snail curry

Ghonghi (freshwater snail) is one of the most loved delicacies of the Tharu community. It is also eaten by the Maithil and other communities in the southern plains. Freshwater snails are found abundantly during the rainy season in ponds, small rivers, canals, and rice fields. The succulent *ghonghi* flesh is perfectly complemented by spices. Flaxseed *(aalash)* adds a nutty flavour to the dish and thickens the curry.

1 kg *ghonghi*
2 tablespoons garlic paste
1 tablespoon ginger paste
1 medium-sized onion
3–4 tomatoes
1 teaspoon turmeric powder
1 teaspoon cumin powder
1 teaspoon coriander powder
1 teaspoon red chilli powder
2 tablespoons flaxseed powder
2–3 bay leaves
2–3 tablespoons mustard or any vegetable oil
Salt as per taste
A handful of fresh coriander leaves, for garnishing

*Serves 3–4 people

The *ghonghi* need to be washed several times before cooking to remove mud and impurities. To clean the *ghonghi*, they are often left overnight in water mixed with a tablespoon of coarse rice flour or grits.

Cut and remove the pointy bottom of the *ghonghi* with a knife. This will get rid of its guts. Clean them thoroughly with water and boil them fully submerged in a pot for around 20–25 minutes. This will further remove impurities and tenderise the meat. Remove from the water. Then, remove the thin disc-shaped protective layer and wash again.

Heat 2–3 tablespoons of vegetable oil in a pan. Add the bay leaves, ginger and garlic paste, and finely sliced onions. Once they start to turn brown, add the turmeric powder and chopped tomatoes. Add the cumin, coriander, and chilli powder. Cook for about 5–6 minutes or until the tomatoes become soft.

Add the boiled *ghonghi*, stir the mixture properly, while adding the salt and flaxseed powder. Then add about 2 cups of water and cook it for about 10–12 minutes.

Turn off the heat and sprinkle some finely chopped coriander leaves for garnishing. Serve with rice or roti. The meat is usually sucked out of the snail, but one can also use a toothpick to get the flesh out of the shell.

ARIKANCHAN

Fried taro leaves filled with lentil paste

The taro plant—indigenous to South Asia—is a versatile vegetable. All of its parts—stalk, tuber, and leaf—are edible and can be made into various dishes. *Arikanchan*, also known as *khariya* or *patushni*, is made by layering a few layers of taro leaves with a black legume-spice paste. The leaves are then rolled into a cylindrical shape and cut into slices. Gram flour, black lentils, and sometimes rice flour are used to make the paste. Taro leaves are delicious to eat, and when fried, have a crispy texture. *Arikanchan* is also made into a curry by cooking it with yoghurt and spices.

10–12 young taro leaves
1 cup black lentils
3–4 tablespoons rice flour, optional
1 tablespoon ginger and garlic paste
1 teaspoon cumin powder
1 teaspoon coriander powder
½ teaspoon of turmeric powder
½ teaspoon of chilli powder, optional
2 cups mustard oil, or any other vegetable oil
Salt as per taste

*Serves 3–4 people

Soak the black lentils overnight. Remove the outer layer of the lentils by rubbing them with the hands and washing them. It's not necessary to remove them completely.

Clean the fresh taro leaves and place them in the sunlight for a few hours to wither, or just leave them for a day. Be careful while handling uncooked taro leaves as they irritate the skin.

Grind the soaked black lentils into a paste using a mortar and pestle or an electric grinder. Add the ginger and garlic paste, turmeric, cumin, coriander, and chilli powder (optional), rice flour (optional), and salt to the paste. Mix well.

Lay a withered taro leaf on a table or a plate and spread 2–3 tablespoons of the paste evenly. Layer another taro leaf and spread the paste again. Continue the process until 3–5 layers are placed. Then roll them tightly into a cylindrical shape. They are easier to roll when withered.

Steam the rolls for about 10–12 minutes and let them cool. They become firm once cool. Cut them into 1–2 centimetres thick slices and shallow fry them, preferably in the mustard oil, for a couple of minutes on both sides. The *arikanchan* is now ready and can be eaten as a snack.

BIRIYA

Sun-dried lentil paste and greens nugget

Biriya is sustenance food for the eastern Tharu community. Unlike in the mountainous regions where greens are stored for the winter and dry seasons, the Tharus preserve greens for monsoon when the farmlands are flooded, and greens are hard to find. Greens such as lamb's quarters *(bethey saag)*, grass peas *(keshadi)*, amaranth greens *(latte saag)*, broadleaf mustard greens *(rayo saag)*, and mustard greens *(tori saag)* grow abundantly during the winter season. These greens are made into *biriya* by mixing them with black lentil paste and sun-drying them for preservation. The process is similar to *masyaura*, but unlike round-shape *masyaura*, *biriya* has an elongated shape. The greens also ferment slightly during the sun-drying process, which gives them a peculiar tangy flavour. Alternatively, gram flour *(besan)* can be used instead of black lentils. It is consumed by simply deep-frying or making it into a curry.

Biriya
1 ½–2 kg *bethey* or *tori saag*
1 cup black lentils
1 teaspoon salt

Biriya Curry
A handful of sun-dried *biriya*
1 medium-sized onion
4–5 garlic cloves
1 thumb-sized ginger
1 teaspoon cumin seeds
1 teaspoon coriander seeds
3–4 dry red chillies
½ teaspoon mustard seeds
½ teaspoons turmeric powder
½ teaspoon salt
3–4 tablespoons mustard oil

*Serves 2–3 people

Soak the black lentils overnight. Wash the greens. Let them wither in the sun for half a day.

After the lentils are fully soaked overnight, drain the water and grind them into a paste.

In a large pot, add the withered greens, black lentil paste, and salt. Mix them well so that the greens are thoroughly coated in the paste. The paste adds protein and helps to hold the greens together.

Take a few greens coated in the paste, and roll them into elongated shapes to make *biriya*. Do the same with all of the mixture.

Place them in a large tray or *supo* (a round traditional bamboo mat), and let them dry for about 3–4 days under direct sunlight. They can then be stored for several months. *Biriya* can be simply deep-fried in vegetable oil and eaten as a snack, or made into a curry like any other vegetable.

To make *biriya* curry

Grind together the cumin and coriander seeds, garlic cloves, ginger, and red chillies with a tablespoon of water to make a thick spice paste.

Heat a pan over medium heat. Add the mustard oil and fry the mustard seeds. Finely slice the onion and add to

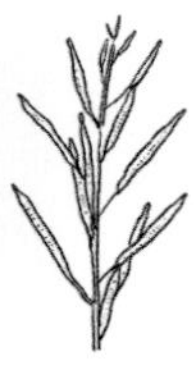

the pan. Fry until light brown and then add the turmeric powder and spice paste. Cook until the spice paste becomes light brown. Crumble the *biriya* with the hands, add to the pan, and fry for about a minute. Add the salt and then 2–3 cups of water. Cook with the lid on for about 10–12 minutes and the *biriya* curry is ready.

SIDHARA

Dried fish and taro stem cake curry

Sidhara, also called *masular*, is an indigenous food prepared from dried small fishes and taro or colocasia stems. The fishes are collected from nearby rivers and ponds, and then sun-dried. The dried fish are first pounded together with taro stems, and then made into a disc-shaped cake and hung outdoors for several days to sun-dry. The cakes can be stored for several months and are usually eaten when fresh vegetables and fish are not readily available.

Fermentation during the drying process imparts a slightly pungent and umami flavour to the dish. It can be an acquired taste, but those who are used to eating this delicacy find it delectable. It can be cooked as a curry or soup and eaten with rice or roti. Like many other indigenous ethnic communities, the Tharus have ingenious ways of preserving food when in abundance for later use during the monsoon or the dry seasons. Other marginalised indigenous communities like Musahars and Danuwars living in the inner Tarai and the Chure range also eat *sidhara*.

Sidhara
1 cup small dried fishes,
5–6 taro/colocasia stems
1 tablespoon turmeric powder

***Sidhara* Curry**
1 large *sidhara* cake
A handful of sun-dried radish, optional
1 medium-sized onion
2–3 garlic cloves
1 small thumb-sized ginger
2–3 fresh green chillies
1 teaspoon red chilli powder
1 teaspoon turmeric powder
2–3 tablespoons mustard oil
Fresh coriander leaves, for garnishing
Salt as per taste

*serves 3–4 people

Peel the outer fibrous layer of the taro or colocasia stems, and cut the stems into small pieces.

Pound the dried fish, taro stem pieces, and turmeric powder together using a mortar and pestle to form a coarse paste.

Fashion the paste into a disc-shaped cake a couple of centimetres thick. Place under sunlight for about 5–6 days. When completely dry, it can be stored for several months.

To make *sidhara* curry

First, soak the dried radish slices in warm water.

Heat about 2–3 tablespoons of the mustard oil in a pan. Finely slice the onion and green chillies, and fry them in hot oil. Also make a garlic and ginger paste and fry until soft. Then add turmeric powder.

Break the *sidhara* into small pieces, put them into the pan, and fry them for about 2–3 minutes. Then add the soaked radish pieces and salt, and cook for a couple of minutes. Add 2–3 cups of water and cook for another 12–15 minutes with the lid on. Garnish with the fresh coriander leaves when cooked.

KATNAUSI

Dry-cooked meat and offal with blood

Katnausi, a dish eaten during the Maghi festival, is prepared from pork (preferably of local pig) or goat meat, along with offal, blood, and spices. There is a ritual in Tharu culture of killing a pig just before the day of Maghi, a practice known as *jeeta marne*. It is believed to be inauspicious to kill animals during Maghi. There is also a tradition of cooking many festive dishes, including tubers, a night before the festival. *Katnausi* is generally prepared as a snack for the people involved in butchering the pig and is a prized delicacy.

600–800 gm pork with fat, including internal-organs like liver, kidney, heart, lungs, etc.
2 cups pig blood, preferably fresh
3–4 *tejpatta* (bay leaves)
1 medium-sized onion, optional
4–5 garlic cloves
1 thumb-sized ginger
3–4 green chillies
1 teaspoon cumin powder
1 teaspoon coriander powder
1 teaspoon turmeric powder
1–2 tablespoons vegetable oil
Salt as per taste

*serves 3–4 people

Cut the meat and offal into small, bite-sized pieces.

Grind the garlic and ginger together to make a paste. Finely slice the onion and chop the green chillies.

Heat 1–2 tablespoons of vegetable oil in a pan or wok, add the bay leaves, garlic and ginger paste, finely sliced onion, and chopped green chillies. When the ginger-garlic paste and the onion turn light brown, add the turmeric powder. Add the fatty meat pieces and fry them for around 3–4 minutes to melt the fat.

Then add the rest of the meat, including the offal, and cook for 15–20 minutes, stirring occasionally. Add the cumin and coriander powder, and some salt in between.

When the meat is light brown, add the blood and stir. In case the blood is clotted, use your hands to break the clots apart and add them to the cooking meat. Cook by stirring occasionally for another 12–15 minutes. It is important to use some fat or fatty meat as it imparts a rich flavour to the dish. The blood gives an earthy metallic flavour.

The dish is usually eaten with roti, puffed rice or beaten rice, and home-brewed alcohol.

TARUWA

Deep-fried vegetable fritters

A popular snack in the Tharu and Maithil communities, *taruwa* is prepared during festivals and celebrations, and also when there are guests in the house. It is basically deep-fried vegetable fritters coated with gram flour and/or rice flour batter. *Taruwa* means 'deep-fried in oil', and any kind of vegetable can be used. It is usually served as a snack or a side dish with the main meal. Here is a recipe with some commonly used vegetables.

Vegetables
250 gm cauliflower
250 gm ladies' fingers
250 gm brinjals
250 gm potatoes
250 gm large-size chilli or pepper
½ litre mustard oil or any other vegetable oil, for frying

Batter
1 cup *besan* (gram flour)
3–4 tablespoons rice flour, optional
1 tablespoon ginger and garlic paste
1 teaspoon cumin powder
1 teaspoon coriander powder
½ teaspoon turmeric powder
½ teaspoon chilli powder
1 teaspoon nigella seeds
1 teaspoon salt

*serves 3–4 people

Take the gram flour and rice flour (optional) in a large bowl and add all the spices including salt and nigella seeds. Add about one and a half cups of water and make a batter. The batter shouldn't be too thick or runny. The rice flour adds texture and a crunch to the dish.

Clean and slice all the vegetables into bite-sized pieces (or any size preferred). But make sure that they are about the same size, so that they all cook evenly.

Place the sliced vegetables in the batter and mix them together so that each piece is nicely coated.

Heat about half a litre of vegetable oil in a deep frying pan. When the oil is hot enough, fry a small batch of vegetables at a time for about 8–10 minutes. Fry them in batches as crowding the pan will lower the temperature of the oil and make the fritters soggy. Use a perforated spatula to take the fritters out of the oil. Serve them hot, preferably with tomato or mint/coriander achaar.

MACHHKA JHOR

Fish curry

Fish is an important source of protein for communities living in Nepal's southern plains. It is, in fact, an intrinsic part of their food culture as they inhabit the banks of large rivers and flooded plains. Fish are cooked into soups or curries, fried, and also dried for later use. Fish dishes are essential food items prepared during the festivals.

Fish curry is usually made with mustard seed paste and spices. *Rohu* fish, a kind of carp, is the preferred variety of fish because of its flavour. The curry tastes better the next day as the fish absorb all the flavours from the soup.

1 kg freshwater fish, preferably *rohu*
3–4 medium-sized tomatoes
1 medium-sized onion
2–3 green chillies
6–8 garlic cloves
1 thumb-sized ginger
1 tablespoon mustard seed paste
½ teaspoons mustard seeds
½ teaspoon fenugreek seeds
½ teaspoon black pepper
1 tablespoon *garam masala*, optional
1 tablespoon cumin and coriander powder mix
3–4 tablespoons mustard oil
1 lemon/lime
Fresh coriander leaves, for garnishing
Salt as per taste

Marination
1 teaspoon turmeric powder
1 tablespoon vegetable oil
1 lemon/lime
Salt as per taste

*serves 3–4 people

Cut the scaled, gutted, and cleaned fish into one-inch-thick pieces. If the fish are small, cook them whole after removing the scales and the guts.

Add the vegetable oil, turmeric powder, salt, and lemon juice to the fish pieces. Mix them well to ensure that the pieces are coated thoroughly with spices. Let them marinate for about 30 minutes.

In a pan, heat about 3–4 tablespoons of mustard oil. When the oil is hot, fry the fish pieces on both sides until they turn light brown. Transfer the fried fish pieces into a plate.

In the remaining oil, fry the fenugreek and mustard seeds. When the seeds start popping, add the finely chopped onion, fresh chillies, finely minced garlic, and ginger. Fry until they are soft and light brown. Add the turmeric powder and finely chopped tomatoes, mustard seed paste, and salt to taste. Cook the tomatoes for about 4–5 minutes, or until they melt completely. Then add the cumin and coriander powder, black pepper, and *garam masala* (optional). Give a good stir and cook for another 6–8 minutes, or until the oil and spices start separating. Add a few tablespoons of water in between to prevent burning.

Add about 4 cups of hot water and bring to a boil. Then add the fried fish pieces, squeeze some lemon juice, and give the mixture a gentle stir. Cook over low heat for around 10–12 minutes with the lid on. Don't stir vigorously as it will break the flesh. Turn off the heat, gently stir the curry, and garnish with the fresh coriander leaves.

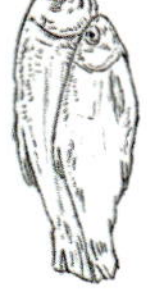

KADHI BADI

Fried gram flour dumplings and yoghurt curry or soup

The Maithils cook *kadhi badi* especially on new year's day Jud Sital, which is an important festival in the Mithila region, and also when sons-in-law and esteemed guests visit. The recipe is made by cooking deep-fried gram flour dumplings or balls in yoghurt or buttermilk and spices. *Kadhi* refers to a 'yoghurt-based soup or curry' and *badi* refers to the 'deep-fried gram flour dumplings'. We also prepare *kadhi* at home, but from vegetables such as bitter gourds and ladies fingers instead of gram flour dumplings. Possibly, the culture of cooking vegetables in yoghurt or leftover buttermilk in hilly Khas communities came from the southern plains, where it is a popular traditional food.

1 cup gram flour
1 tablespoon rice flour
½ cup yoghurt
½ teaspoon fenugreek seeds
½ teaspoon mustard seeds
½ teaspoon cumin seeds
1–2 bay leaves
2–3 dried red chillies
1 teaspoon turmeric powder
1 teaspoon cumin powder
1 teaspoon coriander powder
1 teaspoon red chilli powder
2 tablespoons garlic paste
Salt, according to taste
½ cup mustard oil
Fresh coriander leaves, for garnishing

*serves 2–3 people

For the dumplings, take a cup of gram flour in a large bowl, and add half a teaspoon of turmeric powder, a tablespoon of garlic paste, and about half a teaspoon of salt. Add water gradually and beat it to make a thick batter. The batter must be light and without any lumps. To check if the batter is light enough, add a tiny lump of batter into water. If it floats, the batter is good for making dumplings. Let the batter rest for about half an hour.

In a cooking pot, heat half a cup of mustard oil over medium heat. Make small marble-sized balls or dumplings of batter and drop them into the oil. Fry both sides of the dumplings until light brown. Leave a couple of tablespoons of batter in the bowl to make the soup.

In the same bowl with the leftover batter, add the yoghurt, cumin, coriander, and red chilli powder, garlic paste, salt (to taste), and turmeric powder. Whisk them together until the yoghurt becomes light and creamy. Whisking prevents the yoghurt from splitting. Add about 4 cups of water and mix together.

Remove the excess mustard oil, leaving about 2–3 tablespoons in the same cooking pot that was used to fry the dumplings. Over medium heat, fry the mustard seeds, cumin seeds, fenugreek seeds, dried red chillies, and bay leaves. Immediately add the thin mixture of batter, yoghurt, and spices. When the soup starts to boil, add the fried gram flour dumplings and cook for about 10–12 minutes. Adjust salt if required. Turn off the heat. Garnish with the chopped fresh coriander leaves.

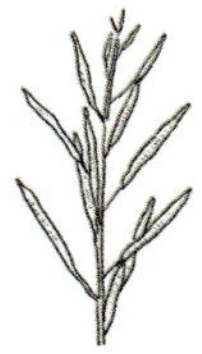

THEKUWA

Deep-fried whole wheat cookie

Sweets constitute an important part of the Maithil food culture. *Thekuwa* is a traditional deep-fried cookie prepared from whole wheat flour, jaggery, milk, and ghee. It is often flavoured with coconut and spices such as cardamom, cloves, or cinnamon. Offered to the gods and eaten as *prasad* (god's offering), it is especially prepared during Chhat, a festival dedicated to the worship of the sun for sustaining life on earth. It is also prepared during the Teej and Jitiya festivals. It comes in various shapes, sizes, and imprints made using a metal or wooden mould.

½ kg whole wheat flour
½ cup jaggery, use sugar as an alternative
4–5 tablespoons ghee
½ cup milk
1 teaspoon cardamom powder
50 gm dried coconut
½ litre vegetable oil or ghee, for frying

Place the jaggery (or sugar as an alternative) and half a cup of water in a pot, and let the jaggery melt over low-medium heat. Turn off the heat, and let it cool.

Take the whole wheat flour in a large bowl, add the ghee, and sprinkle the cardamom powder. Grate the dried coconut and add to the bowl. Mix them well together. Pour about half a cup of milk and the melted jaggery, and mix them together. Knead the mixture lightly to make dough. Let the mixture rest.

While the dough rests, heat half a litre of vegetable oil or ghee in a pan for frying. Take a small portion of dough, give it a round shape, flatten it, and give it an imprint using a metal or wooden *thekuwa* mould. Or one can just make a round shape using the hands. When the oil or ghee is hot enough, fry a few at a time until they turn golden brown on both sides. *Thekuwa* is soft when hot, but becomes crispy and crumbly when it cools. Store the *thekuwa* in airtight containers and it should last for a few weeks.

TILKO LADDU

Sweet sesame seed balls

Tilko laddu (*til:* sesame, laddu: ball-shaped sweets), also known as *tilauri,* is prepared during the Maghi festival. *Laddu* can also be made of puffed rice (known locally as *murai*) and beaten rice. Many dishes eaten during Maghi, including *tilko* laddu, are high-energy foods that keep the body warm during the cold winter season. Sesame seeds hold an important place in Tharu culture and in Hindu religion. They are offered to the ancestors and deities, and sesame oil is used to light lamps during religious activities. Sesame seeds are mostly used as flavouring ingredients in achaars in Nepali kitchens. *Tilko* laddu is a must-have food during the festival in many communities.

1 ½ cups sesame seeds
½ cup jaggery

Roast the sesame seeds in a pan over low-medium heat. Stir continuously while roasting. When the seeds start to pop, put the lid on or they will get all over the place. Roast for 15–20 seconds more with the lid on while continuously shaking or stirring the pan to roast the seeds evenly and avoid burning. Transfer the roasted seeds to a large bowl and let them cool.

Crumble or cut the jaggery into small pieces and cook in a pan over low heat until it melts completely and becomes a little darker.

Pour the melted jaggery over the roasted sesame seeds and mix them together with a spatula to make sure the roasted seeds are nicely coated with the melted jaggery. Do not touch the mixture with your hands. When the temperature of the mixture lowers slightly, enough to be touched comfortably by hand, rub your palms with oil and make small balls out of the mixture. One needs to make the balls as fast as possible, as the jaggery will start to solidify when it cools, making it difficult to fashion into balls.

When the balls cool completely, the *tilko* laddu is ready. They are sweet and crunchy, with a nutty and smoky flavour. The balls can also be stored in air-tight jars for several months.

Sherpa, Tamang, & Tibetan Cuisines

SIMPLE, DELECTABLE FLAVOURS OF THE HIMALAYAS

In the mountainous region, guests are often greeted with a cup of warm *su-cha.* Made by churning *nak* (female yak) butter, salt, milk, and brewed tea in a wooden or bamboo cylinder called a *dong mu*, *su-cha* is drunk all day long to keep the body warm and hydrated in cold climates. While trekking to the Khumbu region in 2009, I remember sitting by the firewood oven and drinking *su-cha* all day long in Khumjung, a small Sherpa village. As the days were already getting colder with the onset of winter, the tea was essential to keep the body warm. Earlier the same year, I had *su-cha* for the first time in a small village in Manang. Not sure if I liked it then, but I love it now. It is an acquired taste. *Su-cha* is more than a drink in mountainous region; it is a tradition.

The Sherpas and Tamangs live at the frontier of the Himalayas: The Sherpas in the Solu and Khumbu regions and the Tamangs largely in the central region. The Tamangs are believed to be the early inhabitants of the Kathmandu Valley, but they now live largely in the surrounding hills and mountains. Some hypothesise that Tamang is derived from the Tibetan words: *ta* and *mag* mean 'horse' and 'rider' respectively. The Sherpas are believed to have eastern Tibetan roots, as the word Sherpa is derived from the Tibetan *shar-pa,* which means 'eastern people'. When the Sherpas migrated from Tibet to the Solukhumbu region, they brought their traditions and culture along. Over time, the Sherpas have developed their own distinct culture and cuisine, resulting from the isolated environment of the region.

Over the years, many Tibetans have also come to Nepal, more recently in the 1960s as refugees, and have resided in Nepal for generations. In many ways, the recipes and ingredients of the Tibetan diaspora have enriched indigenous Nepali cuisines.

In the cold harsh mountain climates, only a limited number of crops grow. Barley, naked-barely, buckwheat, and potato are the primary crops of the region. Maize and millet are cultivated in the lower region. *Sen* (thick porridge-like dish) and *kur* (unleavened bread) are both made from wheat, barley, or buckwheat flour and constitute the primary diet of the Sherpas and also other mountain communities. *Sen* and *kur* are eaten with curry or stew of potatoes, beans, seasonal vegetables, and occasionally, meat. Mountainous cuisine, of both the Sherpas and Tamangs, has simple flavours that mainly come from garlic, chillies, onions, turmeric, and Sichuan pepper (*airmong*).

Barley or naked-barley is soaked, roasted, and ground to make *tsampa,* which holds significant cultural significance for the Sherpas, Tamangs, and communities descended from Tibetans. They use *tsampa* while offering prayers in rituals and festivals. The Sherpas consume *tsampa* on a daily basis by mixing with *su-cha* to make a porridge called *chamdur* or to make a soft dough called *paag.*

Although the potato is not indigenous to Nepal and was only introduced to Khumbu in the mid-19th century, it has since become deeply ingrained in Sherpa cuisine. No other food is as quintessential as potato for Sherpa daily meals. The Sherpas make pancake, mash, stews, curries, dumplings, and even alcohol from the humble potatoes. They also eat boiled potatoes simply with achaar, which is a common mid-day snack for people working in the fields. In the early days, they also dried potatoes and made them into flour.

Animal husbandry is also a big part of the Sherpa livelihood, even though the practice is now declining. They rear yak in the higher altitudes and their cross-breeds in the lower regions for milk, which is then turned into various dairy products. Butter is extracted from yoghurt, and cheese-like whey known as *serkam* is extracted from buttermilk. Fresh or dried *serkam* is used as a flavouring ingredient in achaars and soups. *Serkam* and milk cream are also fermented for months to make pungent, bitter-tasting *somar* and *shoshim,* which are used for flavouring. Butter is largely used to make *su-cha,* mixed with *tsampa,* and also used to light lamps during prayers and puja.

Meat, traditionally, is not a big part of Sherpa food culture, but they consume yak, buffalo, and sheep meat during festivals. As in many others, Sherpa and Tamang communities also preserve meat by sun-drying or smoke-drying for later use. A preserving practice unique to the Sherpas is making *phalgi.* They boil unripe maize and then dry to make *phalgi,* and stock up for winter. This preservation technique retains the sweetness and tenderness of the unripe maize.

The Sherpas, Tamangs, and Tibetans celebrate Lhosar, the new year celebration and the biggest festival, which revolves around family, prayer, and food. The festivities begin by making the most essential food item, *khapsey* (a sweet deep-fried pastry). They consume and offer *khapsey* to gods during the first day of Lhosar. On the eve of Lhosar, families get together and eat a special festive dish called *guthuk,* a soup made traditionally from nine ingredients: bean, barley, dumplings or noodles, meat, chilli, radish, and other vegetables.

Mountainous Himalayan cuisines are simple yet nutritious. Despite the limited crops and produce, the communities have developed culinary means to not just survive the harsh environment but also to diversify the palate.

Sonam Dorjee Gurung

Kur: Thick unleavened bread or roti made from wheat or barley flour.

Syan/Sen: Thick porridge-like dish made from millet, barley, buckwheat, or wheat flour.

Rikikur: Potato pancake/roti traditionally served with *nak* butter and sauce/achaar made from fresh precipitated buttermilk dregs *'serkam'* or fermented *serkam.*

Babar: Deep-fried plain roti made from rice or buckwheat flour batter, a traditional festive delicacy of the Tamang and Hyolmo communities.

Alum: Steamed millet flour dough, a common Tamang dish.

Fulaura: Deep-fried buckwheat flour balls.

Shaphale/Shabhalep: Deep-fried pastry filled with minced meat, spring onion, and spices.

Shyakpa/Thenthuk: Typical Sherpa and Tibetan hand-torn noodle soup with meat, potato, radish, and greens.

Thukpa: Noodle soup with meat and/or vegetables.

Momo: Dumplings filled with minced meat mixed with spices.

Rilduk: Hearty soup made from mashed-pounded potato dumplings.

Phalgi: Winter stew of steamed and then dried unripe maize kernels, often with beans, meat, potato, radish, and carrot.

Guthuk: Stew made from nine ingredients eaten on the eve of *Lhosar* as a festive meal.

Tsampa: Roasted barley or naked-barley flour eaten with butter tea or milk.

Tingmo: Fluffy steamed bun made from wheat flour.

Lhaphing: Tibetan spicy and savoury cold noodle (originally a northern Chinese dish known as *liangfen*).

Gyuma: Blood sausage prepared with minced meat (including offal) of a yak, sheep, or mountain goat, and sometimes including rice or *tsampa*, and encased in intestines.

Goyang: Fermented leaves of wild edible brassica plant.

Chhurpi: Hard cheese made from yak milk.

Serkam: Buttermilk dregs or whey.

Somar and Shosim: Fermented buttermilk dregs and milk cream, respectively.

Chengkol: Fermented barley or naked-barley alcoholic drink mixed with *tsampa*, butter, sugar, egg, and nuts.

RIKIKUR

Savoury potato pancake

The Sherpas love the potato. It is one of their main staples, although it was introduced in the Khumbu region less than 200 years ago. It is eaten almost daily and is used to make various dishes: curry, stew, soup, mashed, dumpling, roti, etc. Boiled potatoes are also simply eaten with a chilli-garlic-salt achaar or sichuan pepper-salt condiment as a snack.

Rikikur is a traditional potato pancake or roti served with *nak* (female yak) butter and achaar. In the Sherpa language, *riki* means 'potato' and *kur* means 'bread or roti'. Potatoes are peeled, grated finely, and mixed with buckwheat flour to make batter, and then cooked in a pan. Earlier, rough or rigged stone surfaces were used to grate potatoes, which were cooked on thick, flat stone slates over firewood. Precipitated dregs or whey extracted from buttermilk, known as *serkam*, is ground together with spring onions or chives, green chillies, and salt to make achaar or dipping sauce. Achaar is also made from fermented *serkam* known as *somar* or fermented milk cream known as *shosim*, which have a strong flavour. *Rikikur* is a simple but energy-rich dish to begin the day with.

Pancake
8–10 medium-sized potatoes
3–4 tablespoons buckwheat flour
5–6 tablespoons nak (female yak) butter, or regular butter

Sauce
½ cup *serkam*, alternatively thick sour yoghurt
2 stalks spring onions
1–2 fresh green chillies
Salt as per taste

* makes about 7–8 *rikikur*

Peel the potatoes, wash, and finely grate. Put the grated potatoes in a bowl, and add 3–4 tablespoons of buckwheat flour for binding. Any other flour available can be used. Add a few tablespoon of water if required and mix them together to form a thick batter.

Put a pan on a stove over medium heat and grease it with *nak* butter. When the pan is hot enough, put about two spatulas of the grated potato batter. Spread the batter evenly using the spatula, giving it a thin round shape. While spreading, dip the spatula in water a couple of times to avoid it sticking to the batter. Cook for about 4–5 minutes until light brown. Flip it over and cook for another 3–4 minutes.

For the achaar or sauce, grind the *serkam* (or thick yoghurt) chopped spring onions, fresh green chillies, and salt together into a fine paste.

Serve the *rikikur* immediately with a tablespoon of nak butter and *serkam* sauce. The *rikikur* tastes better when hot and fresh.

BABAR

Deep-fried rice flour roti

Babar is a traditional festive dish of the Tamang, Hyolmo as well as some Sherpa communities. It is prepared from rice flour, sometimes from buckwheat flour, and is an essential dish during the Sonam Lhosar festival. It is also prepared during special occasions such as weddings. This thin unflavoured deep-fried roti is generally eaten with achaar, curry, or butter tea. Traditionally, bark from a local tree, *daar (Boehmeria rugulosa)*, is added to make the roti soft and fluffy.

2 cups rice
½ litre mustard oil or vegetable oil, for frying

Soak the rice in water for at least 4–5 hours. Drain the rice thoroughly and grind into fine flour. Freshly prepared flour made by soaking and then grinding rice is better.

Put the rice flour in a mixing bowl. Pour about two and a half cups of water into the bowl and mix together to form a runny batter.

Heat the mustard or vegetable oil in a deep frying pan over medium heat. Once the oil is hot enough for frying, turn down the heat to low. Stir the batter, scoop it out with a ladle, and pour it slowly into the oil without interruption. It will form a round shape and float to the top once it is cooked. Let it fry for another minute and take it out with a slotted or perforated spatula. Continue with rest of the batter. Serve hot with a curry, achaar, and/or butter tea.

Note: Due to the heat of the oil, the first *babar* may not turn out smooth.

RILDUK

Potato dumplings soup

I had *rilduk* for the first time in a Sherpa eatery tucked away in an alley in Boudha, Kathmandu, which is an area settled by a large number of mountainous communities, including the Sherpas and Tibetans. Locals and visitors frequent this small eatery for a cup of *su-cha* or some Sherpa dishes. Served hot in a bowl with *airmong* (sichuan pepper) grounds and chilli sauce, these potato dumplings were so light that they floated in the soup and were soft enough to melt in your mouth.

Mountain potatoes are boiled and then pounded heavily in a *tsomgok*, a large wooden mortar and pestle, until they become a soft and silky lump. To make *rilduk*, they are then made into small dumplings and served in a simple soup made from onions or spring onions, garlic, chillies, and *airmong*. In some communities, boiled potatoes are simply mashed into a paste known as *rilduk sen* and served in large lumps like *dhindo*. Traditionally, the soup is flavoured with *shosim* (fermented buttermilk dregs or milk cream). It is pungent and has a bitter taste, but it makes the soup delicious when used in small amounts.

½ kg potatoes
A small handful of spring onions or chives
1 small onion
1–2 green chillies
4–5 garlic cloves
½ teaspoon turmeric powder
½ teaspoon red chilli powder, optional
½ teaspoon *airmong* grounds
½ teaspoon *shosim*, optional
1–2 tablespoons vegetable oil or preserved-animal fat *(tsiluk)*
Salt as per taste

*Serves 2–3 people

Wash the potatoes and boil them until they are well-cooked. Let them cool and peel the skins off. Moisten a mortar and pestle with water, and add the peeled potatoes. Mash the potatoes and then pound until they turn into a completely soft and silky dough, without lumps. Moisten the pestle occasionally to prevent sticking.

Chop the onion and spring onions. Make a coarse paste of garlic and green chillies.

To make the *rilduk* soup, heat 1–2 tablespoons of vegetable oil or preserved fat in a cooking pot over medium heat. When the oil is hot enough, add the chopped onion and garlic-chilli paste. Fry until they become aromatic and light brown. Add turmeric powder and chopped spring onions or chives. Then add salt, *airmong*, and red chilli powder, and pour in about three cups of water. Add a couple of tablespoons of *serkam* or half a teaspoon of *shosim* if available.

When the soup starts to boil, turn off the heat. Moisten your hand, take a small lump of pounded potatoes, squeeze to make small dumplings, and drop into the soup. The *rilduk* is ready. Sprinkle some chopped spring onions and *airmong* grounds.

SHYAKPA

Hand-torn noodle soup with meat and vegetables

Shyakpa, also known as *thenthuk* in the Tibetan language, is a typical Sherpa and Tibetan hand-torn noodle soup. This hearty, comforting, nutritious soup is eaten during winter to keep the body warm and provide much-needed nutrition. The noodle soup is generally made from winter vegetables, dried meat, and freshly made noodles. In the Sherpa language, *shyakpa* means meat soup: *shya* is meat and *pa* generally denotes stew or soup. *Thenthuk*, which is derived from the Tibetan language, translates to hand-torn noodles: *then* means pull and *thuk* means noodles. Every household has its own way of making *shyakpa*.

Soup

300 gm of lamb, goat, yak or buffalo meat-with bones, preferably smoke-dried meat
1 medium-sized radish
1 medium-sized carrot
2–3 medium-sized potatoes
1–2 spring onions
1 medium-sized onion
2–3 tomatoes
3–4 garlic cloves
1 thumb-sized ginger
½ teaspoon black pepper
½ teaspoon *airmong* (Sichuan pepper)
½ teaspoon turmeric powder
1 teaspoon red chillies powder/flakes
2–3 tablespoons vegetable oil
1 lemon
Salt as per taste

Noodles

1 cup wheat flour
About ½ cup water

*serves 3–4 people

Heat two tablespoons of vegetable oil in a pot or pressure cooker. Add chunks of bone-in meat, which is the secret to make flavourful broth. Cook with an occasional stir until the meat becomes light brown. If using smoke-dried meat, soak it first for 15 minutes before cooking. Then, add the roughly chopped onion, smashed garlic and ginger, spring onions (save some for garnishing later), diced tomatoes, turmeric powder, and salt to taste. Then pour about five cups of water, put the lid on and cook until the meat is tender. It will take about 20–25 minutes in a pot and 2–3 whistles in a pressure cooker.

Prepare vegetables while the broth is cooking. Slice the potatoes, carrot, and radish.

Once the meat is cooked, add some water and bring it to a boil. Then add the finely sliced potatoes, radish, and carrot to the broth.

Mix wheat flour and water and knead it to make noodle dough.

Rub your hands with the oil, take some dough, make an elongated shape using the thumb and index finger, and pinch the tip of the dough to flatten it. Pull it to the desired length and add into the broth. Repeat the process until all the dough is used up. Try making noodles of an even thickness so that they cook at the same time. Depending on the size of the vegetable slices and

the thickness of noodles, cook for around 8–10 minutes. Add a handful of spinach at the end. Turn off the heat. The *shyakpa* is ready to serve.

Sprinkle some *airmong* grounds and chilli powder and garnish with the finely chopped spring onions. Also squeeze some lemon juice to the noodle soup. Eat it hot.

PHALGI

Hearty winter stew of steamed and dried unripe maize with beans

Around the end of summer, when the maize is still in the milk-stage (unripe and sweet), they are harvested, boiled or steamed, and then dried for a few days to preserve for winter. These steamed-then-dried unripe maize are known as *phalgi makai*. The process helps to retain their sweetness and tenderness, both of which are otherwise unavailable in mature, dried maize. The dried maize are then processed: kernels taken off the cob, pounded to break them into half, sieved to remove the outer layer, and stored.

Sherpa and other neighbouring communities, mainly living in the lower mountainous region, make a hearty winter stew out of this maize, known as *phalgi*, which is cooked together with butter beans (*seto simi*), meat, and vegetables such as radish and potato that are widely grown in the mountainous region. For many Sherpa people living outside their homelands, this is a dish that evokes nostalgia. Fresh or smoke-dried meat of sheep, buffalo, or yak is used for the stew. Radish is a key vegetable and is used in stews and noodle soups, which imparts a delicious flavour to the dish. For an authentic taste, try using local varieties of maize and beans grown in the mountainous regions.

1 cup processed *phalgi makai*
1 cup butter beans
400–500 gm meat or 150 gm dried meat
1 medium-sized radish
3–4 potatoes
1 thumb-sized ginger
5–6 garlic cloves
2–3 green chillies
1 teaspoon red chillies powder
½ teaspoon *airmong* (Sichuan pepper)
1 teaspoon turmeric powder
2–3 tablespoons vegetable oil
2–3 spring onion stalks
Salt as per taste

*serves 3–4 people

Soak processed *phalgi makai* and beans separately for at least 4–6 hours or overnight. Do not throw away the water that the kernels are soaked in, as it will be added to the soup.

Place the soaked *phalgi makai* and beans in a pressure cooker, add about two cups of water, and cook over medium heat for about 3–4 whistles (about 15–20 minutes).

If adding dried meat, soak it first in hot water for about 15 minutes and cut into bite size pieces.

In a pot, heat 2–3 tablespoons of vegetable oil. Pound garlic cloves, ginger, and chillies together, and fry them in the oil. Add turmeric powder and chopped bone-in meat. Cook the meat for about 10–12 minutes (3–4 minutes, if dried meat) with an occasional stir until it turns light brown. Add the cooked *phalgi makai* and beans. Add salt and then pour 2–3 cups of water, including the water that the *phalgi makai* were soaked in.

Once the stew starts to boil, slice potatoes and radish, and add them to the stew. Sprinkle some chilli powder and *airmong* grounds. Let the stew simmer over low heat for about 15–20 minutes until the meat and vegetables are fully cooked. Adjust salt if required. Turn off the heat and serve hot in a bowl garnished with the chopped spring onions. Sprinkle more *airmong* grounds if preferred.

KHAPSE

Deep-fried pastry

Khapse is a deep-fried pastry made from wheat flour, butter, and sugar. It is crispy, buttery, and slightly sweet, usually eaten with butter tea as breakfast or a snack. It is a cultural dish of mountainous communities, and is especially prepared during the Lhosar festival and ceremonies like weddings. Mounds of *khapse* arranged beautifully are also placed at religious shrines as an offering during the festival.

3 cups plain wheat flour
½ cup butter, preferably yak butter
2–3 tablespoons sugar
½ cup milk
1–2 eggs, optional
½ teaspoon salt
2–3 cups vegetable oil, for frying

In a large bowl, mix together the flour, eggs (optional), butter, milk, and about a half cup of water. Knead the mixture to form a dough. Let it rest for about half an hour. Divide the dough into 2–3 balls.

Sprinkle some flour over a rolling board, place a ball of dough, and roll into 2–3 mm thick sheets using a rolling pin. Cut the sheets into rectangular shapes, each about an inch wide and a couple of inches long. Next, make a small incision in the middle of the rectangle using the tip of the knife. Fold one end of the rectangle through the cut to give it a twisted traditional shape as shown in the illustrations. *Khapse* can also be made into various other shapes.

In a deep pan, heat the vegetable oil (or ghee) over medium heat. Once the oil is hot enough, fry the twisted pastries. Using a spatula, pour hot oil over the *khapse* to make it crispier. Flip the *khapse* over and fry until both sides are light brown.

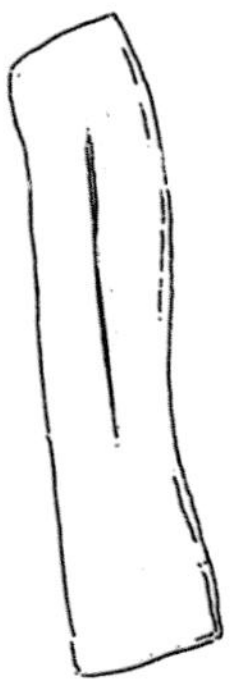

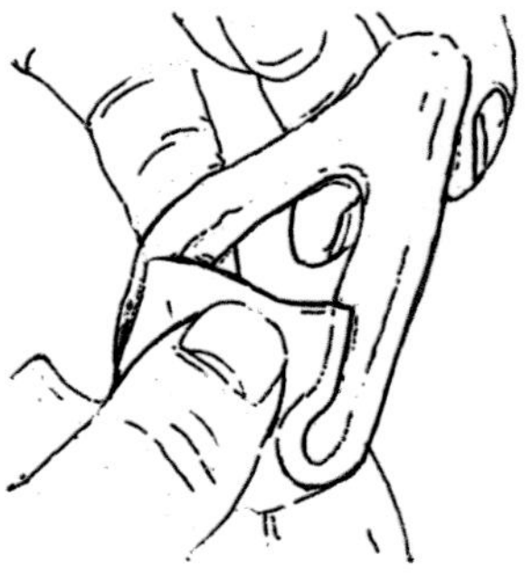

MOMO

Meat or vegetable dumpling

Momo is undoubtedly the most popular food in Nepal, especially in urban areas. Momo is a dumpling filled with minced meat, vegetables, herbs, and spices, and served with achaar. It originally came from Tibet, but has been adapted to local tastes using indigenous ingredients and spices. Many ethnic groups have their own ways of making momo. The kind prepared by the Sherpa and Tibetan communities living in Nepal is very similar to the Tibetan momo. Yak or sheep meat is traditionally used, but one can use pork, chicken, or buff to make momo. For vegetarians, cabbage, carrot, spring onion, chive, and potato can be used.

Momo filling

500 gm minced meat with some fat
1 tablespoon garlic paste
1 tablespoon ginger paste
2 medium-sized onions
2–3 spring onions stalks
Salt as per taste
2–3 tablespoons vegetable oil

Dough

2 cups of wheat flour
1 cup of water
1 tablespoon vegetable oil

*serves 3–4 people

To make the momo filling, place the minced meat including the fat in a bowl. Finely chop onions and spring onions, and add to the minced meat, along with ginger and garlic paste and salt. Pour a tablespoon of vegetable oil, and mix them together.

To make the dough, take flour in a large bowl, drizzle a tablespoon of vegetable oil and add water. Mix them together and knead well to make soft dough. Leave it to rest for about 15–20 minutes covered with a moist cloth.

Sprinkle some flour over a rolling board to prevent sticking. Take a small marble-size ball of dough and roll using the rolling pin to turn it into a thin round-shaped wrap about 5–6 centimetres in diameter.

Once done making wraps, fill each wrap with a tablespoon of filling and enclose by folding the tip of the wrap making pleats and pinching at the ends, as shown in the illustrations. One can form any desired shape or pattern.

Grease the steamer before placing the dumplings to avoid sticking. Steam the dumplings for about 12–15 minutes. Serve hot with freshly made spicy tomato achaar.

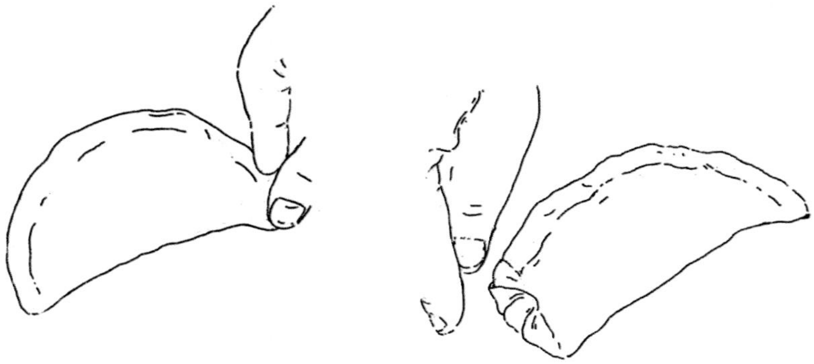

SHAPHALE

Deep-fried minced meat pastry

Shaphale or *shabhale—sha* means meat and *phale* means bread in the Tibetan and Sherpa languages—is a deep fried pastry filled with minced meat. This crispy soft pastry with meat filling is usually served with chilli sauce. *Shaphale* came with the Tibetan diaspora in the 1960s and 1970s, and has now become a popular street food in Kathmandu and around areas inhabited by Tibetans.

Filling
300 gm minced meat, including fat
2–3 stalks spring onions
1 tablespoon minced ginger
1 tablespoon minced garlic
1 medium-sized onion, finely chopped
½ teaspoon black pepper grounds
1 tablespoon soy sauce, optional
About 1 teaspoon salt
1 tablespoon vegetable oil

Dough
2 cups wheat flour
1 tablespoons vegetable oil or butter
A pinch of salt
1 cup water

Chilli sauce
A handful dry red chillies, large ones with less heat
½ teaspoon *airmong* (Sichuan pepper)
2 garlic cloves
A pinch of salt

Frying
About a cup of vegetable oil

*makes 6–8 *shaphale*

To make the *shaphale* filling, mix minced meat (including some fat) with the minced ginger and garlic, finely sliced onions and spring onions, black pepper grounds, salt, and vegetable oil in a bowl. Mix them well using the hand.

To make the dough, add the flour, salt, butter, and water in a large bowl. Mix them together and knead the dough. Leave it to rest for about 15 minutes.

Divide the dough into 6–8 pieces. Take a piece of dough, make it into a round ball and flatten by hand. Sprinkle some flour on the rolling board and the dough to prevent sticking while rolling. Roll into a round shape of a diameter of 4–5 inches. Add about 2–3 tablespoons of filling on one half of the dough wrap, leaving some space on the edges to enclose. Lightly wet the edges with water, and fold the other half over. Press the edge all around to enclose, then slightly pull the edges using the thumb and index finger, twist and fold over, making pleats, and repeat up to the other end, creating a pattern as shown in the illustrations.

Heat about a cup of vegetable oil in a pan. Fry them one at a time over medium heat. Pour the hot oil over the exposed surface of the *shaphale*. When the surface submerged in the oil turns light brown, flip over and fry until the other side also turns brown. It should take about 3–4 minutes to cook each side.

Serve the *shaphale* hot with chilli sauce. To make the sauce, first soak dry chillies in hot water for about 10 minutes to make them soft, and then grind together with the garlic, Sichuan pepper, and salt to form a paste.

Magar & Gurung Cuisines

ETHNIC FLAVOURS FROM THE GANDAK HILLS

When young, my Magar friends taught me how to identify and catch *paha* (Himalayan freshwater frog). During summer weekends and holidays, we would go to the nearby river to swim and fish. I remember barbecuing fish and *paha* by the riverside. I grew up close to a Magar community and got to experience their culture.

The Magars and Gurungs largely inhabit hilly areas in the Gandak region. Magar settlements are generally in the lower mid-hills while Gurung settlements are located at much higher altitudes. Both live in dense and closely-knit settlements built on terraces. The Gurungs also practice a transhumant way of life, which is moving along with their herds of sheep to pastures at higher altitudes during summer and descending to lower altitudes during winter. This practice, however, has declined significantly now.

The Magars and Gurungs mainly cultivate millet, which grows easily in the less fertile soil and without the need for irrigation. Its flour is used to make *dhindo* (thick porridge-like dish) and roti, which are traditionally part of the daily meal. They ferment millet grains using *marcha* (yeast) to make *jaand* (fermented millet alcoholic drink) and *raksi* (distilled millet liquor), which are essential in rituals, festivals, celebrations, and for hospitality. The Gurungs living in higher elevations also cultivate buckwheat and foxtail millet. The Magars also cultivate maize, a key component of their diet. Maize kernels are roasted for mid-day snacks while maize flour is cooked as *dhindo* and grits are cooked as rice. They also cultivate rice in areas where irrigation is accessible. A variety of rice *(ghaiya)*, which doesn't require irrigation, was once grown, but its cultivation has almost been abandoned.

For special occasions of the Magar community such as Maghi and weddings, *batuk* (deep-fried black lentil patties), meat of the local black hog, and alcohol are essential. During the weddings, the groom's family takes these items to the bride's family. Boiled yam and taro, and *selroti* (deep-fried roti made from rice

flour batter) are also consumed during festivals. *Jhilinge* roti or *khiuni*, made by pressing cooked rice paste into thin stringy noodles, is a festive food of both the Magars and Gurungs. The roti is first sun-dried and later consumed by deep-frying it. Lhosar is the biggest festival of the Gurungs. Other key festivals include Dashain, Tihar, and Poush Pandhra, which are also observed by the Magars. They consume water buffalo, sheep, goat, and rooster meat generously during festivals and occasions.

Tubers such as taro, yam, *ghitta* (aerial yam), and *bhyakur* are traditionally consumed by the Magars. *Sisnu saag* (nettle greens) is a common wild vegetable for both communities and is cooked into a thick soup. Other common wild vegetables eaten by these communities are fiddlehead fern, bamboo shoot, and mushroom.

Indigenous agricultural knowledge and skills have helped the Magars and Gurungs survive in the less-fertile hilly terrain. Their cuisines are thus hardy and nutritious, making the most out of the limited amount of crops they are able to grow, domesticated animals, and produce foraged from the wilds.

Dhindo (Paigo): Thick porridge-like dish prepared from millet or buckwheat flour; a traditional staple of the Magar and Gurung communities.

Aanto: Maize grits cooked as rice.

Kodoko roti: Millet flour pancake.

Batuk: Deep-fried black lentil patties (sometimes prepared from ricebeans); an essential cultural food of the Magar community required in festivals and marriage ceremonies.

Selroti: Deep fried ring-shaped confection or *roti* prepared from rice flour batter and ghee.

Jhilinge roti: *Roti* made by pressing a cooked rice paste into thin stringy noodles, which are then sun-dried and later consumed by deep-frying, a festive delicacy of the Gurungs.

Gundruk ra bhatamaasko jhol/tihun: Dried fermented greens and soybean soup or curry.

Niguroko tihun: Fiddlehead fern curry.

Sisnuko khole: Nettle greens soup.

Usineko tarul: Boiled yam usually eaten as a snack with a chilli-salt paste.

Karelako achaar: Bitter gourd achaar with sesame seed grounds and spices.

Sukako karkaloko achaar: Dried taro stem made into sour, spicy achaar.

Waksya: Local black hog meat curry.

Sukuti: Smoke-dried meat.

Jaand ra raksi (Paa): Alcoholic drink prepared by fermenting millet, sometimes with maize and wheat; an integral cultural drink of the Magars and Gurungs.

AANTO

Cooked maize grits

In earlier days, when rice was not easily available, millet and maize were the major staples of both the Magars and Gurungs. Only a small amount of rice was grown in limited irrigated land and it was usually kept aside for special occasions and festivals. Maize and millet were ground into flour and cooked as *dhindo* and roti. The coarser maize grits were cooked as rice, commonly known as *aanto* or *chyankhlako bhat*. This dish is cooked simply by boiling maize grits in water, and eaten with curry, daal, and achaar. Other hilly communities in Nepal also eat *aanto*, and my mother used to cook it occasionally as an alternative to rice.

2 cups maize grits
1 tablespoon of ghee

*serves 3–4 people

Wash the maize grits to remove any impurities and soak them in water for about 30 minutes.

Add the soaked maize grits and about 4–5 cups of water in a cooking pot or *kasaundi*. Boil over medium heat. Stir occasionally to cook evenly and avoid burning the bottom.

Once the water is almost gone, reduce the heat to low, add a tablespoon of ghee, put the lid back on, and cook further for about 10 minutes. Turn off the heat and let it rest for at least 5 minutes.

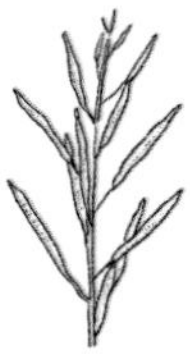

KODOKO ROTI

Millet flour plain pancake

Kodoko roti is a plain pancake or roti made from millet flour. It can be eaten at any time of the day—as breakfast, a midday snack or even as lunch or dinner. It is also widely consumed by other hilly communities. My mother grew up eating it and it is her favourite food. I remember her using talc stone *(khari dhunga)* instead of ghee to make the pan non-sticky for cooking roti. At our home, we often eat *kodoko* roti with dipping sauce made by melting ghee and *khudo* (sugarcane molasses) or honey together.

2 cups millet flour
About 2 cups water
A few tablespoons of ghee

*makes 8–10 rotis

Take the millet flour in a bowl and add water. Whisk them together to make a thick batter. Beat well to bring out the sweetness and get rid of any lumps.

Heat a thick-base pan over medium heat. Smear the pan with half a teaspoon of ghee. When the pan is hot, pour about half a cup of batter and spread using the hand or a ladle. Give it a round shape with even thickness. Put the lid on (clay lid is better) and cook the roti until the moisture is gone. Then flip the roti and cook for another couple of minutes. It should take around 6–8 minutes in total. Continue the process until all the batter is used up.

BATUK

Deep-fried black lentil patties

Batuk is the most essential cultural food of the Magars. It is a small ring-shaped deep-fried patty prepared from black lentil paste mixed with spices. Typically, only ginger paste, salt, and turmeric powder are used as flavouring, but garlic paste, onions, spring onions, green chillies, coriander leaves, and cumin powder can also be added. One can also add finely chopped broadleaf mustard greens in the black lentil paste to make *batuk* even more delicious.

The culture of eating *batuk* is prevalent in many other communities in Nepal, including the Khas community in the far-west. The Newa community calls it *bara*. *Batuk* is considered an ancient food in the Indian subcontinent and its history can be traced back to the first millennium BCE. The name *batuk* is likely derived from *vataka*, an ancient name for the dish in the Dravidian language.

Batuk is one of the primary dishes eaten during Maghe Sankranti or Maghi, the largest festival of the Magars besides Dashain and Tihar, and also prepared during wedding ceremonies. Festive foods items are cooked on the eve of Maghe Sankranti. A similar dish, but of a round, ball-like shape, is known as *fulaura*. In Brahmin culture, *fulaura* is an essential item in the annual death ceremony *(shraddha)* and is also prepared during festivals.

1½ cups black lentils
2 tablespoons ginger paste
1 tablespoon garlic paste
½ teaspoon turmeric powder
1 teaspoon salt
2 cups vegetable oil, preferably mustard oil

*serves 3–4 people

Soak the black lentils in water overnight.

Massage the soaked lentils with hands to separate the outer black layers. Wash several times with water to remove the outer layers, but it is not necessary to remove them completely. Drain the water.

Grind the lentils into a coarse paste using a grinder or food processor. Traditionally, the grinding is done in a mortar and pestle. A slightly coarse paste makes the *batuk* fluffier and gives it texture.

Transfer the lentil paste to a large bowl. Add the ginger paste, garlic paste, turmeric powder, and salt for flavour, and mix them all together. The mixture needs to hold together; if required, add a couple tablespoons of water to make it moist.

Heat about two cups of vegetable oil in a deep frying pan over medium heat.

Moisten your hand with water to avoid sticking, take a small handful of the mixture, and make a small doughnut-

shaped patty with a hole in the centre. When the oil is hot enough, drop a few of the patties into the oil. Fry until both sides are light golden brown. Each side will take around 4–5 minutes. Use a skewer or slotted spoon to flip the *batuk* and take it out of the oil. Do the same with the remaining lentil paste and fry them in batches. *Batuk* is generally eaten with pork or vegetable curry, yoghurt, or tea.

KAGUNOKO KHIR

Sweet foxtail millet pudding

My mother tells me that her parents used to grow *kaguno*, also called *kauno*, when she was young. It was grown in *khoriya*, a sloping portion of less-fertile land made by clearing bushes and trees. With rice slowly taking over as the preferred staple grain, nutritious grains such as *kaguno* (foxtail millet), *chino* (*proso* millet), *phapar* (buckwheat), and *junelo* (sorghum) are being increasingly neglected, and people have stopped farming these grains in most areas. These grains are usually grown in the mid-hills and can easily be cultivated in arid, less-fertile regions. *Kaguno* is a traditional crop grown in the Karnali region, in the far west of Nepal, also grown by the Chepangs in the mid-hills and the Gurungs in the lower Himalayan region.

The grain can be simply cooked as rice, and also be made into khir and *jaand*. Its flour is made into roti and *dhindo*. Traditionally, the Gurungs make khir and special alcoholic drinks out of *kaguno*. It makes a soft and creamy khir, one of the best I have had.

1½ litre milk
½ cup *kaguno* (foxtail millet)
3–4 cardamom
2–3 *tejpatta* (bay leaves), optional
2 tablespoons sugar
2–3 tablespoons honey

*serves 3–4 people

Heat one and a half litres of milk in a pot. Add the crushed cardamom and sugar. Bring it to a boil.

When the milk starts boiling, wash the *kaguno*, add it to the milk, and cook over low-medium heat for around 30–40 minutes. Stir the mixture occasionally to avoid burning the bottom. After about 30 minutes, the pudding should turn thick and creamy. One can eat it hot or cold with a variety of toppings: honey, fruits, berries, nuts, etc.

TAREKO TARUL

Pan-fried yam with spices

A key sustenance food for the Magar community, *tarul* (yam) is indigenous to the South Asian region. A few varieties of yam are cultivated while others are foraged from the wild. *Ban tarul* (wild yam) is considered a prized delicacy as it is not readily available and difficult to dig out of the ground.

Growing up close to the Magar community, I remember going to Maghe Sakranti, Thulo Ekadashi, and Chaite Dashain fairs as a kid and eating *tareko tarul* and other boiled root vegetables. Such fairs used to be a big affair in the past, but they have all disappeared now.

1 kg *tarul* (yam)
1–2 tablespoon cumin seeds
1–2 red chillies
5–6 garlic cloves
Large thumb-sized ginger
1 teaspoon turmeric powder
1 teaspoon salt
1 tablespoon vegetable oil
3–4 tablespoons ghee or vegetable oil, for frying

*serves 3–4 people

Boiled yams are generally eaten by dipping them in a salt and green chilli paste. They can also be mixed with spices and pan-fried with some ghee or oil to make a crispy snack, which is different from traditional ways of eating yams, like boiling them or making a curry.

Boil or steam a whole yam over low-medium heat until cooked. Boiling takes around 30–40 minutes in a pot or about 15–20 minutes in a pressure cooker, depending on the size of yam. Let the boiled yam cool before peeling off the skin and cutting it into slices a centimetre thick.

Grind together the cumin seeds, chillies, garlic, ginger, and salt to make a fine paste. Apply the paste as well as turmeric powder and vegetable oil to the yam slices. Let them marinate for at least 15–20 minutes.

In a pan, add a few tablespoons of ghee or vegetable oil and shallow-fry each side of the yam slices for around 2–3 minutes. Eat this spicy fried yam hot.

SISNUKO KHOLE

Nettle greens soup

Young leaves and flowers of the stinging nettle, known as *sisnu* in the Nepali language, are widely consumed by indigenous ethnic communities living in the hilly and mountainous regions. This wild, herbaceous, perennial flowering plant has tiny, stinging hairs that need to be dealt with care. *Dhindo* or *chyankhlako bhat* (cooked maize grits) and *sisnuko khole* (thick nettle greens soup) make for a simple peasant's dish that is a good source of energy and nutrition.

Greens, including nettle greens, have always been seen as a humble vegetable that commoners or peasants eat. This is even depicted in the tragic epic *Muna Madan*, which was adapted from an 18th century Newa folk song by the great Nepali poet Laxmi Prasad Devkota. Devkota's epic narrates the tragic story of an impoverished man forced to leave his family for work in Lhasa, Tibet. In one particular couplet, Madan's wife Muna pleads with her husband to not leave for Lhasa:

> *Hataka maila sunaka thaila ke garnu dhanale*
> *Saag ra sisnu khayeko besa anandi manale*
>
> (What's to be done with sacks of gold that are but dirt off the palm
> It's better to eat greens and nettles with a heart full of content)

400–500 gm young nettle greens
1 teaspoon ginger paste
1 teaspoon garlic paste
1–2 garlic cloves, finely chopped
1 teaspoon turmeric powder
2–3 tablespoons maize flour, or of any grain
½ teaspoons *timmur* (Nepali pepper) grounds
3–4 green chillies
1 lemon
2 tablespoons ghee or vegetable oil

*Serves 3–4 people

Wash the nettle greens thoroughly in water using tongs to avoid the stinging hairs.

Take about 3–4 cups of water in a large pan or *karai* and bring to a boil. When the water starts boiling, add the young nettle greens using a pair of tongs and cook for about 6–8 minutes with the lid on. Then add the ginger paste, garlic paste, *timmur* grounds, salt, and flour, and cook with an occasional stir for about 15 minutes with the lid on, or until the greens become soft. Traditionally, a wooden device called *firke* is used to mash the greens, but they can also be mashed with a spatula. Squeeze half a lemon's juice into the soup, stir, and take off the heat.

On a small saucepan, heat about two tablespoons of ghee or vegetable oil for tempering the spices. Fry garlic and turmeric powder, and pour the mixture over the nettle greens soup. Give it a good stir and serve the soup with a fresh green chilli. It can be eaten with roti, rice, or *dhindo*.

GUNDRUK BHATMASKO JHOL

Fermented greens and soybean soup

Gundruk, sun-dried fermented radish greens and broadleaf mustard, is a cross-cultural food. It is usually eaten as soup or achaar. *Gundruk* and soybean soup is a common dish in the hilly regions and is consumed by many communities, including the Magars and Gurungs. The soup was traditionally prepared during the dry season, when fresh vegetables were difficult to find. It can be consumed as an alternative to daal and curry, and eaten with rice, roti, or *dhindo*. The peculiar sour flavour from the fermented greens is what makes the soup delicious.

1 bowl or a big handful of *gundruk*
½ cup soybeans
1 medium-sized onion
2–3 garlic cloves
1 small thumb-sized ginger
3 medium-sized tomatoes
1 teaspoon cumin and coriander powder
½ teaspoon turmeric powder
2 fresh red chillies
½ teaspoon fenugreek seeds
½ teaspoon mustard seeds
Fresh coriander leaves, for garnishing
1 lemon
2 tablespoons of mustard oil, or any vegetable oil
Salt as per taste

Soak the *gundruk* in hot water for about five minutes.

Heat a cooking pot over medium heat. Roast the soybeans for 4–5 minutes, stirring continuously until they crack and turn light brown. Transfer the roasted soybeans to a bowl.

In the same pan, heat about two tablespoons of mustard oil or any vegetable oil. When the oil is hot, fry the fenugreek and mustard seeds. When the seeds start popping, add the chopped onions, minced ginger, minced garlic, and halved green chillies, and fry until light brown. Add the turmeric powder. Drain the water and add the *gundruk* to the pan. Saute for about two minutes while stirring occasionally. Add tomatoes and cook until they soften. Then add roasted soybeans, cumin and coriander powder, and salt. Stir well.

Add about 3–4 cups of water and bring to a boil. Reduce the heat to low, put the lid on, and cook for around 8–10 minutes. Squeeze some lemon juice. Turn off the heat and garnish with the fresh coriander leaves.

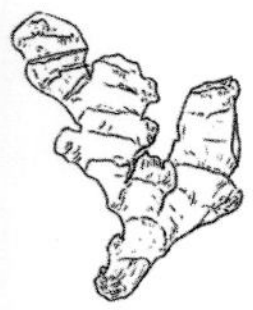

WAKSYA

Local pig meat curry

Meat from the *sungur* (local domestic pig) holds an important place in the food culture of the Magar community. It is essential to every festival, ceremony, and celebration. The groom's family is traditionally required to take a whole pig, along with alcohol and other food items, to the bride's house as a gift during the wedding ceremony.

Bone-in and skin-on pork is cooked together with basic spices to make a curry.

1 kg pork, bone-in meat from a pig or a wild boar with the skin and fat
1 medium-sized onion
3–4 tomatoes
1 tablespoon garlic paste
1 tablespoon ginger paste
1 tablespoon cumin and coriander powder
1 teaspoon red chilli powder
1 teaspoon turmeric powder
2 tablespoons vegetable oil
Fresh coriander leaves, for garnishing

Cut the bone-in meat, including the fat and skin, into bite-sized pieces.

Heat about two tablespoons of vegetable oil in a cooking pot with a thick base. When the oil is hot, add the pork pieces and a teaspoon of turmeric powder. Fry the meat for about 10–12 minutes or until the meat turns light brown. Stir occasionally. First, the meat will release some water, and later, the fat will render. Scoop out some of the fat if preferred.

Push the meat to one side to make some space in the pan to fry the spices. Add the chopped onions and then the ginger and garlic paste. Fry until they turn light brown. Mix them together. Then add the salt, cumin and coriander powder, red chilli powder, and chopped tomatoes. Give the mixture a stir. Once the tomatoes soften, add half a cup of water, and cook for another 15–20 minutes over low-medium heat with the lid on. Stir occasionally. Turn off the heat and garnish with the roughly chopped fresh coriander leaves.

AALU SUKUTIKO TARKARI

Potato and smoke-dried meat curry

This simple yet delicious curry is often cooked and consumed by Gurung herders while taking their livestock to the highlands during summer. Potatoes and smoke-dried meat (*sukuti*) can be stored easily for months and carried to faraway sheds, which may be located a day or a couple of days away from the nearest settlement.

Meat from buffalo, sheep, or mountain goat is smoke-dried over a fire for several hours to make *sukuti. Sukuti* is largely prepared during festivals when there is abundant meat. In the early days, hunting was common, and *sukuti* was also made from game meat. It provides much-needed protein and also gives a delicious flavour to any dish. This particular curry is typically eaten with *dhindo,* rice, or roti.

4–5 medium-sized potatoes
A handful of *sukuti* (smoke-dried meat)
1 medium-sized onion
2–3 medium-sized tomatoes, optional
4–5 garlic cloves
1 thumb-sized ginger
1 teaspoon red chilli powder
1 tablespoon cumin and coriander powder mix
1 teaspoon turmeric powder
2 tablespoons vegetable oil
Salt as per taste

*serves 3–4 people

Soak the *sukuti* in hot water for about 15 minutes to make ing the meat tender and easier to cut. Remove the *sukuti* from the water and cut it into bite-sized pieces. Wash potatoes and cut into cubes.

Heat the vegetable oil in a pan. Add the chopped onion, ginger paste, and garlic paste when the oil is about to smoke. As the spices turn light brown, add the turmeric powder. Then add the *sukuti* and fry for 3–4 minutes. Add the diced potatoes and cook for another 3–4 minutes with the lid on.

Add the cumin and coriander powder, dry red chilli powder, salt, and chopped tomatoes, and cook for another 3–4 minutes. Pour about 3–4 cups of water, preferably hot, and let the curry boil over low-medium heat with the lid on for another 15–20 minutes. The potatoes and smoke-dried meat make for a simple yet delectable curry.

Khas Cuisine

CUSTOMARY FOOD FROM THE MID-HILLS

Dashain and Tihar are my favourite times of the year. When young, my siblings and I would wait for the festivals with great excitement as they brought holidays, new clothes, gifts of cash, get togethers with families, and most importantly, festive food items. My mother would make varieties of festive rotis: *selroti*, *khude* roti, and colourful *jhilinga* roti. We also participated in the laborious work of rolling dough for *fini* roti. As a half Bahun household, Dashain would not be complete without goat meat. Every year, during the eighth day of Dashain, goats are sacrificed to the goddess Durga across the country, and the resulting goat meat is cooked into a variety of dishes. Lean meat is usually cooked as a curry or dry-cooked to make *pakuwa;* offal is cooked together with blood to make *bhutuwa;* bone-in meat is cooked into a soup or stew; and any surplus meat is smoke-dried for preservation. Fresh liver roasted over firewood ember is a treat during Dashain. These meat dishes are generally eaten with festive rotis, beaten rice, and the fermented cucumber achaar made especially for the festival. Dashain and Tihar are the biggest festivals celebrated by the Hindu Khas-Pahadi community.

The term Khas-Pahadi is generally used for the community of the Bahuns, Chhetris, Dalits, and Thakuris, who are now spread across Nepal. Most groups labelled as Khas usually identify themselves with their castes, even though whenever these castes have migrated from their cultural heartlands in Western Nepal, they have been referred to as Pahadi or Parbate, terms that indicate their origins in the hills.

Khas-Pahadi cuisine in many ways is representative of the Hindu culture of Nepal's mid-hills. Food is often categorised into pure *(chokho)* and impure *(bitulo)*. There are even dietary restrictions, like fasting on certain occasions and avoiding meat consumption during Ekadashi, the eleventh day of each of the two lunar phases. Many Khas-Pahadi communities also abstain from consuming alcohol and beef.

Most Nepali households consume *daal-bhat-tarkari,* constituting of cooked rice with lentil soup and curry, twice daily. Rice is the most important grain of the community. It also plays a role in Hindu traditions: it is offered to the gods during the *homa* (a sacrificial fire ritual) and also used in a tika (a mark worn on the forehead for good luck). An important child-weaning ceremony is known as the *bhat khuwai* or 'rice-feeding'. Rice is also used to make varieties of rotis and sweets. *Selroti,* which is prepared by deep-frying rice flour batter into ring-shaped roti, is the most commonly prepared food during festivals and important occasions. *Selroti* is one of the very few festive food items that is consumed across many cultures. The preparations for a marriage ceremony begin with the making of *kasaar*, which is a round aromatic sweet made from roasted rice flour, ghee, and jaggery.

In the Nepal's far west, the Khas-Pahadi community cultivates a wide variety of grains that grow easily in less fertile soil, such as *kaguno* (foxtail millet), *chino* (proso millet), *junelo* (sorghum), and *marse/latte* (amaranth). *Marsi*, a cold-tolerant variety of rice, is grown at elevations of up to 3,000 metres where irrigation is accessible.

Legumes, such as *kalo maas* (black lentil), *gahat* (horse gram), *bhatmaas* (soybean), *siltung* or *masyang* (rice bean), *bodi* (black-eyed pea), and *simi* (bean), constitute a big part of Khas-Pahadi cuisine. Legumes are of particular importance, where multiple dishes are prepared from ground lentils such as *dupka*, *batuk*, and *maasko puri*. *Fulaura*, a deep-fried lentil ball, is an important dish prepared during *shraddha*, the annual death ritual where one pays homage to deceased parents.

Milk and dairy products such as *dahi* (yoghurt), *khuwa* (evaporated milk solids), *ghiu* (ghee), and *mohi* (buttermilk) are essential parts of the culture, and used in many recipes. The dairy culture was passed down from their ancestors who were pastoral nomads. Milk and ghee, especially from cows, are regarded as pure, and are thus used in religious rituals.

The Bahuns are also known for their culture of eating a variety of sweet dishes. Khir (sweet rice porridge) and *puwa* (rice flour cooked in ghee and sugar) are especially prepared during religious ceremonies and festivals. There is even a Nepali quip: *jahan guliyo, tyahan bahun bhuliyo*, remarking that the Bahuns tend to lose themselves in sweets.

Khas-Pahadi cuisine is multi-layered, influenced by history, customs, and religious values. And one that varies moderately across the hills. While the daily staple meals are similar, it is during the festivals and celebrations that the richness of this cuisine can be glimpsed.

Khir: Sweet rice or tapioca pudding cooked in milk with spices and nuts, prepared during festivals and ceremonies.

Dhakani: Sweet rice pudding prepared by cooking an aromatic rice variety in ghee and milk.

Khichadi: Savoury black lentil and rice porridge cooked with ginger and ghee, and eaten during the Maghe Sankranti festival.

Dupka: Thick soup or curry made of black lentil or horse gram paste dumplings, the most popular food of the far-western region of Nepal.

Puwa: Sweet dish prepared by frying rice flour or grits in ghee and sugar.

Chamre and Latte: Sticky or aromatic rice cooked in ghee and sugar. *Chamre* is prepared from an aromatic rice variety and *latte* from a sticky rice variety.
Both are eaten during the Poush Pandhra festival.

Batuk and Fulaura: Deep-fried black lentil patties prepared during the Maghe Sankranti festival; *Batuk* is ring-shaped while *fulaura* is a round ball.

Chhach batuk: *Batuk* (deep-fried black lentil patties) in buttermilk flavoured with spices; consumed by the Khas community in the far-west.

Fini roti: Crispy deep-fried layered pastry prepared from wheat flour and ghee.

Selroti: Deep-fried ring-shaped confection or roti prepared from rice flour batter and ghee.

Khude roti/Arsa: Deep-fried sweet roti prepared from rice flour and sugarcane molasses.

Puri: Deep-fried rice or wheat flour roti made especially during religious ceremonies and festivals. In the far-west, it is often filled with cooked lentil paste.

Makaiko roti: Unleavened maize flour roti often cooked in banana leaves.

KHIR RA DHAKANI

Sweet rice pudding

Khir is a traditional delicacy common among many ethnic communities in Nepal, and also the hill Khas community. It is prepared by cooking rice in milk, sugar, and spices such as cardamom, cloves, and bay leaves. It is prepared during festivals like Teej and Saaune Sankrati and also during pujas or religious ceremonies. As khir is cooked over low heat for a long time, it has a soft and creamy texture.

Dhakani is a traditional festive dish similar to khir, but the rice is cooked in ghee first and has a bit of texture. It is eaten in the hilly areas of the western region, especially by the Khas community. It is usually made with local varieties of aromatic rice, such as *basmati*, *chandanchur*, *jetho-budho*, *pokhreli masino*, *pahele*, etc. *Dhakani* is largely enjoyed during the Teej festival.

Khir

1 cup rice
2 litres milk
4–5 cardamom
5–6 tablespoons sugar
½ cup dry coconut pieces and/or nuts of choice

*serves 3-4 people

Dhakani

1 ½ cups rice, preferably an aromatic rice variety
1 litre milk
4–5 cardamom
5–6 tablespoons sugar
5–6 tablespoons ghee
½ cup dry coconut and/or nuts of choice

*serves 3–4 people

Soak the rice for about an hour and drain.

To make khir

Boil the milk in a cooking pot over medium heat. Add the sugar, crushed cardamom, and rice to the boiling milk. Cook for about 35–40 minutes on low heat until the dish turns into a thick pudding. When the khir is almost cooked, add the finely sliced coconuts and nuts of your choice, such as cashew, pistachio, almonds, etc. Make sure to stir occasionally while cooking so as to avoid burning the bottom.

To make dhakani

Heat a cooking pot with a thick base over medium heat and add about 5–6 tablespoons of ghee. Also, heat the milk in another pot simultaneously. When the ghee is hot enough, add the soaked rice and stir-fry for about 8–10 minutes until it turns light brown. Then add the sugar, crushed cardamom, grated coconut, and dry nuts of your choice, such as cashew, pistachio, almonds, etc. Cook for another couple of minutes and then add about two cups of hot milk. Stir, put the lid on, and cook over medium heat.

When the milk is absorbed, add the remaining hot milk. Stir and cook further until the milk is completely absorbed and the rice is cooked.

KHICHADI

Rice and black lentil porridge

Khichadi is a one-pot savoury porridge made from rice, black lentils, ghee, and a few basic spices. Rice beans, locally known as *siltung* or *masyang*, and mung beans are also used instead of black lentils. The word *khichadi* literally means a mishmash of ingredients cooked together in a pot. The Brahmins and Chhetris, especially from the western hilly districts, celebrate Maghe Sankranti, a solstice festival, by eating *khichadi*, among other festive foods. It is also eaten by many other communities in Nepal and India. I grew up eating the dish, which was usually cooked once a year. It is cooked a day before the festival, as cooking on the day is considered inauspicious.

1 ½ cups rice
1 cup split black lentils *(kalo maasko* daal)
5–6 tablespoons ghee
1 large thumb-sized ginger
1 teaspoon cumin seeds
1 teaspoon turmeric powder
Salt as per taste

*serves 3–4 people

Wash the split black lentils and rice separately to remove impurities. Soak the lentils for at least a couple of hours and the rice for half an hour. Drain the water.

Boil about 4–5 cups of water separately in a pot.

Heat a *kasaundi* or pressure cooker and add 4–5 tablespoons of ghee. When the ghee melts and is hot enough, add the turmeric powder. Then add the soaked black lentils and rice. Give the mixture a stir so that the rice and lentils are coated with ghee. Add 4–5 cups of hot water (about three cups if using a pressure cooker), the crushed ginger, and about a tablespoon of salt. Stir, put the lid on, and cook over medium heat for about 30 minutes (or for 4–5 whistles in the pressure cooker). If the lentils are not cooked, add some more hot water and cook for longer. Once the lentils are cooked and all the moisture is gone, turn off the heat and let it rest for at least 8–10 minutes with the lid on.

In a small saucepan, heat about two tablespoons of ghee and fry the cumin seeds. Immediately pour over the *khichadi*. Mix them with a spatula. Serve the *khichadi* hot with achaar, milk, or plain yoghurt.

MADA

Rice pancake or roti

Mada is a pancake or roti prepared simply from a rice flour batter. It is a common and popular food consumed by the Khas community of the far western part of Nepal such as Doti, Baitadi, and Dadeldhura districts. Layered *mada* is known as *tale mada*. Sometimes, yoghurt and sugar are also mixed with the rice flour to make a sweet fluffy *mada* known as *faune mada*.

2 cups rice flour, finely ground
3–4 tablespoons *ghee*

Take the rice flour in a bowl and add a tablespoon of ghee, and about two cups of water. Whisk them together to make a thick batter. Leave it to rest for about 15 minutes or so.

Heat a pan over medium heat and grease it with some ghee. When the ghee is hot enough, add a ladle of rice flour batter and spread it into a round shape of even thickness. Cover with a lid and cook for about 4–5 minutes. When the moisture is gone and the bottom of the roti becomes light brown, add a teaspoon of ghee over the roti, flip, and cook further for 2–3 minutes. The *mada* is ready.

To make layered *mada,* known as *tale mada*, add another layer of batter over the roti. Put the lid on and cook. Continue the process one more time. One can add even more layers. Flip the layered roti and cook further for a couple of minutes. The *mada* can be eaten with achaar, curry, yoghurt, or simply with honey.

LATTE

Sweet sticky rice

Latte is a traditional sweet dish prepared from *anadi* rice, the only local variety of sticky or glutinous rice grown in Nepal. Cultivated mainly in the western plains, its production and consumption has been decreasing in recent decades. As new hybrid variants of rice are widely cultivated because of their high yield, indigenous varieties such as *anadi* have become rarer. *Anadi* rice holds a significant cultural value, especially among the Tharu community. Even though most of their lands are now cultivated with new varieties, they still allocate small plots to grow *anadi* rice in adequate quantities for the festivals. Various other local delicacies such as *chichar*, *poka*, *khatte*, *siraula*, *selroti*, etc., are made from the rice, including alcoholic drinks. People believe that the rice has medicinal value, and is consumed with the water that the rice is soaked in.

Latte is mainly consumed during the Maghe Sankranti, Saune Sankranti, and Pandhra Poush festivals by the western hilly communities, including the Khas. Prepared by cooking soaked *anadi* rice in ghee, sugar or molasses, and fenugreek seeds, the dish is characterised by a soft-sticky texture, sweet flavour, and the aroma of ghee and fenugreek. There is also a tradition of feeding this energy-dense nourishing dish to postnatal mothers.

2 cups *anadi* rice
3–4 tablespoons ghee
1 teaspoon fenugreek seeds
4–5 tablespoons sugar or *khudo* (sugarcane molasses)
3–4 tablespoons grated dried coconut, optional
Hot water

*serves 4–5 people

Soak the *anadi* rice for at least two hours or overnight in water and then drain the water.

Heat a cooking pot with a thick base over medium heat. Add 4–5 tablespoons of ghee, and fry the fenugreek seeds and dill seeds. As soon as the seeds start popping, add the soaked rice. Stir the rice gently, making sure every grain is coated with ghee. Cook for 4–5 minutes with the lid on. Stir the rice and add about 4–5 tablespoons of sugar, or according to taste. Traditionally, sugarcane molasses are used instead of sugar.

Lower the heat and cook for another 20–25 minutes in its own steam by covering with the lid. Stir occasionally and add a few tablespoons of hot water if required to prevent burning. The process of cooking a good *latte* is to let the rice cook in its own steam.

When the rice is almost cooked, add some grated coconut to impart more flavour to the dish. Turn off the heat once the rice is cooked. *Latte* can be eaten as a snack on its own or with achaar.

KASAR

Roasted rice flour and jaggery sweets

Kasar is an essential sweet prepared in wedding ceremonies of the Brahmin, Chhetri, and Dalit communities. Prior to the wedding ceremony, a day is assigned to make *kasar*, where family, relatives, and neighbours come together to make it, a cultural custom known as *kasar batarne*. It is prepared from roasted rice flour and jaggery, and flavoured with spices like cardamom and cloves. Jaggery imparts sweetness and holds the rice flour together.

3 cups rice
1 cup jaggery
10–12 cardamom pods
6–8 tablespoons ghee

Soak the rice for at least 3–4 hours or overnight. Drain the water completely and grind the rice to make flour. It is not necessary to make the flour very fine.

Heat a large wok over medium heat. Add the ghee and when it is hot enough, add the rice flour. Roast the flour while continuously stirring until it turns light brown. Transfer to a large bowl or *supo* (bamboo tray). Grind the cardamom into a powder, sprinkle over the roasted flour, and mix them together.

In a pan, add the jaggery and a few tablespoons of water. Cook over low heat, stirring frequently, for about 10–12 minutes or until the jaggery melts completely. Then pour the melted jaggery slowly over the roasted rice flour and stir continuously with a ladle to mix them well. Let the temperature of the mixture cool enough to comfortably touch by hand. Make the mixture into small balls and let them cool down completely. Make the balls as quickly as possible before the jaggery solidifies and becomes impossible to mould. These *kasar* balls can be easily stored for a couple of weeks or more.

KADI

Buttermilk curry or soup

In hilly regions, buttermilk left over after the extraction of butter is made into a deliciously sour soup known as *kadi*. Generally prepared by cooking buttermilk together with sun-dried or fresh vegetables and spices, *kadi* is often consumed as a simple alternative to daal and curry. It's the dish for people in a hurry. My working mother would often make this dish with sun-dried bitter gourd and ladies' finger, or sometimes just with onion. As many households have now stopped churning butter, it isn't a common dish anymore. Instead of buttermilk, one can use regular sour yoghurt by adding water for a thinner consistency.

1–2 fresh bitter gourds, or a handful of dried bitter gourd slices
6–7 ladies' fingers, or a handful of dried ladies' finger slices
5–6 cups buttermilk *(mohi)*
1 large onion
3–4 garlic cloves
1 small thumb-sized ginger
1–2 green chillies
1 teaspoon cumin and coriander powder mix
½ teaspoon turmeric powder
½ teaspoon red chilli powder
½ teaspoon fenugreek seeds
½ teaspoon cumin seeds
2–3 tablespoons vegetable oil
A handful of fresh coriander leaves, for garnishing
Salt as per taste

*serves 4–5 people

Cut the bitter gourds and ladies' fingers into thin circular slices. Finely chop the onion, slice the chillies into half, and make ginger and garlic paste. If using sun-dried vegetables, soak them in hot water for about five minutes.

Heat a cooking pot over medium heat. Add the vegetable oil, and fry the cumin and fenugreek seeds. Then add the chopped onion, chillies, and ginger-garlic paste. Fry until they become aromatic and light brown. Add the turmeric powder and then the bitter gourd and ladies' finger slices. Cook for about 6–8 minutes with an occasional stir. Add salt, cumin and coriander powder, and red chilli powder. Give it a stir and cook for another minute. Then add the buttermilk. Bring the soup to a boil. Turn off the heat and garnish the *kadi* with fresh coriander leaves.

DUPKA

Lentil paste dumpling soup

A sought-after dish of the Khas community in the far-west Nepal, *dupka* is a thick soup made out of black lentil or horse gram dumplings or balls. Lentils make up a large part of the far-western food culture, as they are made into a variety of dishes, such as *batuk*, *fulaura*, *puri*, and soups or daal.

1 cup black lentils or horse grams
4–5 garlic cloves
1 thumb-sized ginger
1 teaspoon cumin powder
1 teaspoon coriander powder
2–3 dry red chillies
1 teaspoon fenugreek seeds
1 teaspoon turmeric powder
1–2 tablespoons rice flour
1 tablespoon *jimbu* (wild Himalayan allium)
1 tablespoon ghee
2–3 tablespoons mustard oil
1 lemon/lime
Salt as per taste

*serves 3–4 people

Soak the lentils overnight.

The next day, drain the water and grind the soaked lentils together with the garlic, ginger, cumin and coriander powder, and dry red chillies into a paste. Traditionally, a flat stone mortar and pestle is used for grinding.

In a cooking pot, heat 2–3 tablespoons of mustard oil over medium heat. Fry the fenugreek seeds until they pop and add the turmeric powder. Then immediately add about two tablespoons of lentil paste and cook for a couple of minutes. Then add the salt and pour about four cups of water. When the water starts to boil, moisten your hand, take a small amount of the lentil paste and make small dumplings or balls, and add to the soup. Sprinkle rice flour and cook for about 20 minutes until the dumplings are cooked thoroughly.

Heat a tablespoon of ghee in a small pan, fry the *jimbu*, pour immediately over the soup. Squeeze the lemon, give a stir, and the *dupka* is ready to be served with rice or roti.

GAHATKO DAAL

Horse gram soup

Many Nepali communities have a tradition of eating *gahat* soup at least once every winter, something we follow in our home. This nutritious lentil is believed to have medicinal properties that help ward off the cold in winter. *Gahat* is an important food among many communities and regions: from Tamangs in the mid-hills, Khas in the foothills, to Tharus living in the plains. In the far-west, some communities roast *gahat* first before making it into soup, locally known as *gatani*. The lentil is also used to make *dupka* and filling for *puri*. During Gaura Parva, the largest festival in the far-western region, a mixture of five seeds—one of which is *gahat*—is offered to the gods.

1 cup *gahat* (horse gram)
3–4 garlic cloves
½ teaspoon turmeric powder
2–3 dry red chillies
2 tablespoons *ghee*
1 tablespoon *jimbu* (wild Himalayan allium)
Salt as per taste
1 lemon
Fresh coriander leaves, for garnishing

*serves 3–4 people

Wash the *gahat* to remove any impurities and soak overnight.

In a cooking pot, preferably a pressure cooker for quick cooking, add the soaked *gahat* and about two cups of water (add about four cups if cooking in a regular pot). Add the salt, turmeric powder, and a tablespoon of ghee. Put the lid on and cook for 45–50 minutes in a cooking pot or 20–25 minutes in a pressure cooker (or until 4–5 whistles), over medium-low heat.

After the *gahat* is cooked, add about 2–3 cups of water and bring to a boil. Adjust salt if required. Remove from the heat.

In a small pan, heat a tablespoon of ghee for tempering spices. When the ghee is hot enough, add the finely sliced garlic, dry red chillies, and *jimbu*. Turn off the heat and pour over the soup immediately. Garnish with some chopped fresh coriander leaves, squeeze lemon juice, and eat with rice or roti.

CHUKAUNI

Boiled potato and yoghurt salad

Chukauni is a yoghurt-based potato salad that is believed to have originated in Palpa, a hilly district in the western region. A sour yoghurt is used to make the dish, and the name probably comes from the word *chuk* (concentrated lemon juice), literally meaning *chuk*-like sour tasting. It is consumed in Palpa and the adjacent Gulmi and Butwal. The dish is mainly prepared during festivals and celebrations, and best eaten with freshly made *batuk.*

5–6 medium-sized potatoes
1 ½ cups sour yoghurt
1 small red onion
2–3 fresh green chillies
1 teaspoon roasted cumin powder
A few stalks of fresh coriander leaves
Salt as per taste

Tempering spices
½ teaspoon fenugreek seeds
½ teaspoon turmeric powder
2–4 dry red chillies
2 tablespoons mustard oil, or regular vegetable oil

*serves 3–4 people

Boil the potatoes until cooked. Peel off the skins, cut or break them into bite-sized pieces, and put in a bowl.

Add the yoghurt to the potatoes. Finely chop the onion, green chillies, and coriander leaves, and add to the bowl. Also sprinkle the salt and roasted cumin powder.

To temper the spices, heat two tablespoons of mustard oil in a small pan. Fry the fenugreek seeds, dry red chillies, and then turmeric powder. Turn off the heat and immediately pour the mixture over the potatoes. Mix all the ingredients well and the *chukauni* is ready.

KANCHO MEWAKO ACHAAR

Green papaya achaar

Green papaya is mostly used to make achaar in the hills. The achaar is commonly prepared during Dashain as well as other religious ceremonies and festivals, and eaten as a relish with roti, rice and *puwa*. It is an easy dish to make for large gatherings. Green papaya is also eaten with a dipping sauce made from salt and *chuk* (concentrated lemon juice). It has a crunchy texture and pairs well with *chuk* and fresh lemon juice.

1 medium-sized green papaya
4–5 fresh green/red chillies
1 teaspoon fenugreek seeds
1 teaspoon cumin seeds
1 teaspoon mustard seeds
1 teaspoon turmeric powder
1 teaspoon *chuk* or 3 tablespoons fresh lemon juice
3–4 tablespoons vegetable oil, preferably mustard oil
Salt as per taste

Remove the skin of a green papaya and cut into quarters. Scoop out the seeds. Shred or grate the papaya using a grater.

In a pan, heat about 2–3 tablespoons of vegetable oil (preferably mustard oil) over medium heat and fry the fenugreek, mustard, and cumin seeds. Once the seeds start to pop, add the turmeric powder, chopped fresh chillies, and the shredded/grated green papaya. Give it a stir and then add the salt and *chuk* or lemon juice. Cook for a minute, stirring frequently. This will slightly wither the papaya, but retain its colour and crunchiness.

Author's Flavours

CROSS-CULTURAL FOOD I GREW UP WITH

I started helping my mother in the kitchen before I can even remember how old I was. Growing up in a nuclear family with a working mother, it was usual for us, the children, to help her with the cooking. In Hindu households, menstruating women aren't allowed in the kitchen as they are perceived to be impure during their time of the month. During my mother's period, I would often cook the basic *daal-bhat-tarkari*, following my mother's instructions. The first dish I learnt to make was probably freshly ground tomato achaar, which is my favourite and a must-have relish with any main meal.

Growing up a dual-culture kid, Newa and Brahmin, I got to experience and embrace two different, and oftentimes contrasting, customs. My family practiced both traditions and food cultures in our home, despite the fact that some Newa cultural food practices would be considered unacceptable in Brahmin culture, such as the consumption of buffalo meat and the drinking of alcohol. We enjoy both goat and buffalo meat at home, and consume alcohol as *sagun* (auspicious food).

The everyday meal at home is what a typical Nepali household in the western hill community eats twice a day: *daal-bhat-tarkari*. Occasionally, we eat millet flour roti, *dhindo* (thick porridge-like dish), or *aanto* (cooked maize grits) instead of rice. Unlike the Newas of the Kathmandu Valley whose staple is rice, my mother's Newa community in the hills of western Nepal, in Tanahun, mainly grows and consumes finger millet. During religious ceremonies or when there are guests at home, delicacies such as *ghiu bhat* (rice cooked in ghee), *puwa* (rice flour or rice grits cooked in ghee and sugar), and khir (sweet rice porridge cooked in milk) are prepared.

Special rotis and delicacies are only prepared during festivals and occasions. In the early days, *jhilinge* roti—noodle-like colourful roti made out of rice flour—was made at home, but now, they are bought from the market. Making *jhilinge* roti is a laborious process. Rice was soaked overnight, drained, and pounded to make flour. The flour was then cooked in boiling water while stirring continuously to form a thick dough, which was then stuffed into a moulding machine and pressed to form noodle-like strings. These strings were formed into a few layers of discs, put into a bamboo mat, sun-dried, and stored. It is consumed by deep-frying.

As in many other households and communities, *selroti* (a deep-fried ring-shaped roti made out of rice flour batter) is typical festive fare. *Fini* roti (a deep-fried layered pastry made from wheat flour) is prepared during Tihar. I love eating them the next morning with tea. *Khude* roti (a sweet roti prepared from rice flour and sugarcane molasses) is one of my favourites. As sugarcane molasses is now hard to find, commercially available jaggery is used instead.

Growing up, meat was the occasional festive treat, especially during Dashain and Tihar. Goat and buffalo meat were bought in large quantities to last the entire festival. During these festivals, when meat is abundant, we also smoke-dry meat to make *sukuti*, one of the most beloved Nepali foods. *Sukuti* can be stored for a long period of time. At *mamaghar* (maternal uncle's home), buffalo meat *sukuti* especially of bone-in meat was often cooked with ripe pumpkin, a dish I was not particularly fond of when young because of the pumpkin's sweetness. Now, I love it. Mountain goat meat was a rare delicacy available only during Dashain. A couple of days before the main festival day, my mother would ferment a local variety of Nepali cucumber, known as *bhadaure kankro*, to make achaar that would help ease the digestion after the especially hearty festival meals.

Many recipes and ingredients we used then are not as common as they used to be. I remember eating maize flour roti cooked in banana leaves, millet flour roti dipped in a melted molasses and ghee dip, and *gwarcha* (millet flour dumplings in black lentil daal). *Bhotamari* (a thin crispy deep-fried roti prepared from steamed and then sun-dried rice flour batter), which was made at *mamaghar* during Dashain and Tihar, is now rare. All those simple dishes and festive foods that I grew up eating fill me with a sense of nostalgia, and provide me with great admiration for the diverse food culture that I grew up with.

GHIU BHAT

Ghee flavoured rice

In the past, rice was a luxury that not many people could afford for daily consumption. *Ghiu bhat* was thus an occasional delicacy. My mother used to make *ghiu bhat* for special occasions and when there were guests over. A flavourful dish, it is easy to make. Ghee and fenugreek seeds impart a rich and aromatic flavour to the rice.

2 cups rice
4–5 tablespoons ghee, or butter
1 teaspoon fenugreek seeds
4 cups boiling water

*serves 3–4 people

Soak the rice for about 30 minutes in warm water and drain the water. Soaking makes the rice soft and fluffy.

Boil about four cups of water separately.

Heat a *kasaundi* or a thick-base cooking pot over medium heat. Add the ghee and then fry the fenugreek seeds. As soon as the seeds start popping, add the soaked rice. Cook the rice over medium heat for about 3–4 minutes, stirring occasionally. It will soak up all the ghee. Then add about four cups of hot water, stir, put the lid on, reduce the heat to low, and cook for another 15–20 minutes. Stir a couple of times. Once the rice is cooked and the moisture is gone, turn off the heat and let it rest for about five minutes before serving.

PUWA

Sweet snack made of rice flour and ghee

Puwa is a traditional sweet snack prepared from coarsely ground rice flour. It can be made from maize and semolina flour too. At our home, *kanika* (broken rice or rice grits), produced when the rice grains are milled to remove the husk, is also made into delicious *puwa*. The dish is often offered as a *prasad* (god's food) during Hindu ceremonies.

1 ½ cups rice
1 teaspoon fenugreek seeds
1 teaspoon dill seed, optional
4–5 tablespoons ghee, or butter
3–4 cups boiling water

*serves 3–4 people

To make rice flour, soak rice for 4–5 hours, drain the water, and grind the rice into coarse flour. Or simply use pre-made rice flour. Freshly made flour from soaked rice makes softer *puwa*.

Boil about 3–4 cups of water separately.

In a thick-base pan, heat 4–5 tablespoons of ghee over medium heat. When the ghee is hot enough, fry the fenugreek and dill seeds. Then add the rice flour. Stir continuously until the rice flour turns light golden brown. This takes around 3–4 minutes. Another way to make *puwa* is to first make a thick paste of rice flour with water instead of directly adding flour, and then frying in ghee. If using *kanika*, soak in water for at least half an hour and then fry in ghee.

Add sugar, cook for a couple of minutes, and then pour in about half a cup of boiling water. Stir and cook for about 3–4 minutes with the lid on. Repeat this process a couple of times until cooked. One doesn't need to add water if using rice flour paste.

Turn off the heat when the moisture is gone, and the flour dish becomes fluffy and with small lumps. Ghee, fenugreek seeds, and dill seeds lend flavour and aroma to the dish.

MAKAIKO ROTI

Maize flour roti cooked in banana leaves

Maize is used to make a variety of dishes. Roasted maize kernels *(bhuteko makai)* and popcorn are eaten as breakfast or a midday snack. Maize flour is used to make *dhindo* and roti, and coarser grits are cooked like rice. *Makaiko* roti is not as common as before. I remember eating the savoury roti cooked in banana leaves when I was young. Banana leaves lend the roti a peculiar flavour and help keep them moist.

2 cups maize flour
1 cup water
3 teaspoons salt
7–8 garlic cloves
3–4 green chillies
2–3 tablespoons *ghee*, or butter
Banana leaves

*makes 6–7 medium-sized rotis

Grind the salt, garlic, and green chillies together to make a paste.

Take the maize flour in a bowl and add half of the spice paste. Slowly pour in water and mix together by hand to form a thick dough.

Cut the banana leaves into the size of the pan and grease with some ghee or butter. Take a small ball of dough and spread it evenly on the leaf giving it a circular shape. Cover with another piece of banana leaf. Continue with all the remaining dough.

Heat a cast-iron pan over medium-low flame. Place the roti-wrapped-in-banana leaf in the pan. Put the lid on and cook for about 4–5 minutes until the banana leaves get slightly burnt. Flip to the other side and cook for another 4–5 minutes. This nutritious roti can be eaten with the spice paste made earlier from salt, garlic, and green chillies.

KHUDE ROTI

Sweet rice flour and sugarcane molasses roti

Khude roti is prepared from *khudo* (sugarcane molasses) and rice flour. Prepared during the Tihar festival, it is one of my favourite kinds of festive roti. *Khudo* is prepared by cooking sugarcane juice for several hours into a thick dark brown syrup. This is a traditional preservation technique and the molasses produced can be stored for several months to a year. It gives the roti a caramelised, smoky, sweet flavour. Melted jaggery can be used if sugarcane molasses is not available. The roti made from jaggery is known as *arsa* roti.

2 cups rice flour
1 cup *khudo*
½ litre oil, for frying

*makes 10–12 rotis

Heat a thick-base pot, add the *khudo* and about one-third of a cup of water. Bring to a boil and reduce the heat to low. Slowly add the rice flour while stirring constantly with a wooden spatula. Cook for about 8–10 minutes, stirring and mashing constantly to form a thick silky paste, like *dhindo*. It requires quite an effort. Turn off the heat and let it cool for 2–3 minutes.

In a deep frying pan, heat about half a litre of vegetable oil over medium heat. While the oil is heating, make the roti: oil your hands and the banana leaves (alternatively, a rolling board), take a small ball of the cooked dough, and flatten on the leaves making a round shape by hand.

When the oil is hot enough, take the flattened dough out of the banana leaf carefully and fry each side for about two minutes. Use a slotted spoon to take the roti out and drain the excess oil.

SELROTI

Deep-fried rice flour roti

Selroti, a deep-fried ring-shaped rice flour roti, is a popular festive delicacy in Nepal. Called as *aatimari* in my mother's Newa language, it is a cross-cultural food. Many ethnic communities across the country make *selroti,* especially during major festivals, religious ceremonies, and celebrations. People also take it as a *koseli* (gift) while visiting relatives. Prepared by deep-frying rice flour batter in vegetable oil or ghee, *selroti* has a brown crispy outer layer and a soft inside.

1 kg rice
3–4 tablespoons *ghee*
2–3 tablespoons sugar
½ litre vegetable oil, for frying

*makes 15–18 rotis

Soak the rice in water overnight or for at least 4–5 hours. Drain the water and grind the rice into flour. Traditionally, *dhiki* (lever-based mill) and *jaanto* (stone grinder) are used for grinding. Sift the flour to separate the coarser particles.

In a large bowl, beat the ghee until white. Then add the sugar and rice flour to the ghee and mix them well using the hand. Slowly add warm water and make a thick batter. Check the consistency; it must not break while pouring. If it breaks, add some more water. If it's too runny, add some more flour. Let the batter rest for at least a couple of hours. Traditionally, the batter is left to rest overnight to ferment slightly.

Heat about half a litre of vegetable oil (ghee is preferred for the flavour) in a deep frying pan over medium heat. Typically, a tiny metal bowl known as *paalcha* is placed in the middle of the pan, immersed in the oil, to guide the shape of the *selroti.* Check if the oil is hot enough by dropping in a tiny bit of batter. If it fries and floats instantly, then the oil is ready. Scoop the batter using the palm or a ladle and pour in a circular motion into the oil. For ease, one can also use a small funnel to pour the batter and a finger is used to control the flow. Deep-fry until both sides of the *selroti* are golden brown. Use a skewer to flip the roti over and take it out of the oil. Each side will take about 2–3 minutes to fry. It may seem easy, but it requires some practice to make perfectly shaped *selrotis.*

Serve the *selroti* with a curry or achaar. It can also be eaten as breakfast or a mid-day snack with tea. It can be stored for a few days.

FINI ROTI

Deep-fried puff pastry

Fini roti is a crispy deep-fried puffed pastry, prepared especially during the Tihar festival. It is essential in marriage ceremonies in the Newa community and is also taken as a *koseli* or *sagun* (gift) to relatives. It is also offered to the gods in religious festivals. The only flavour in the roti is from the ghee. Eating the crispy *fini* roti with tea the next day is an absolute delight.

Dough
1 kg wheat flour
3–4 tablespoons *ghee*
2 cups water
½ litre *ghee,* or vegetable oil

***Satho* (layering paste)**
2–3 tablespoons *ghee*
2–3 tablespoons rice flour

*makes 15–18 rotis

To make dough, take the wheat flour and ghee in a large bowl. Mix them well together by hand. Slowly add water and knead the dough. It shouldn't be very soft or sticky. Cover with a moist cloth or keep in an airtight container and leave for at least 30 minutes.

Meanwhile, make *satho*, a paste used to create layers in the pastry: take the ghee in a bowl and beat vigorously using a spoon or by hand until its colour changes to white and it becomes soft and creamy, and then add the rice flour and beat again to make a thick paste.

Knead the dough once again and cut into two equal halves. In a large rolling board or a table, roll the dough using a rolling pin into a rectangular thin sheet about a milimetre thick. Oil the rolling board and pin to avoid sticking. Cut out the edges with a knife to make a rectangular sheet. Spread a thin layer of *satho* all over the sheet and gently roll it into a tight cylindrical form. Then roll against the board so that the length stretches slightly. Cut the roll into two-inch-long pieces.

Oil the rolling board and pin again. Pinch lightly to close the end of the cut dough pieces. Flatten using the rolling pin and form a rectangular roti. Make two or three parallel incisions at around the centre of the roti, which will help the roti puff up. Repeat the process with the other pieces and the other half of the dough. (To make round fini roti, flatten the cut dough with layers exposed, and roll to round shape.)

Heat half a litre of ghee or vegetable oil in a deep frying pan over medium heat. When the ghee is hot enough, fry the rolled-out roti. Constantly scoop and pour hot oil over

the roti, which helps it to cook and puff up. Unlike other deep-fried rotis, this doesn't require flipping . When it puffs up well, take it out using a slotted spoon and drain off the excess oil. Let it cool before serving, which will make it crispy. *Fini* roti is good with milk tea. Storing it in an airtight container will keep it crisp and fresh for weeks.

SAATU

Roasted grains and pulses flour

Saatu is flour or cereal prepared from roasted mixed grains and legumes such as maize, wheat, soybean, and chickpea. Making *saatu* is an annual tradition at our home. I have been eating it for as long as I can remember. When we, siblings, were young, it was easier for my working mother to serve us pre-made *saatu* for breakfast and an after-school meal. It can be stored for several months and requires no cooking. We usually eat it with hot milk or hot water sweetened with honey, sugarcane molasses, or sugar.

Generally, carbohydrate-rich grains are mixed together with protein-rich legumes to make *saatu* in the hills, whereas high mountainous communities, like Sherpa, Tamang and others, have a culture of eating *tsampa*, which is made from locally grown barley or naked barely. *Saatu* is a nutritious wholesome instant meal and can be eaten at any time of the day. It was considered a peasant's food, but there is also a specific auspicious day known as Akshaya Tritiya in Hindu culture for eating *saatu* (prepared from roasted barley) and *sarbat* (a drink made from honey, sugarcane molasses or jaggery). The day lies in the month of Baisakh, the beginning of the summer season. Eating *saatu* and *sarbat* is believed to help the body cope with the summer heat and replenish it with nutrients.

This is a personal recipe from my paternal grandmother. She uses ghee, sugar, fenugreek seeds, fennel seeds, and sugar to flavour *saatu*. Other spices such as cardamom and cloves can also be added.

½ kg maize
½ kg wheat or barley
½ kg chickpeas or soybeans
5–6 tablespoons sugar
5–6 tablespoons ghee
1 tablespoon fenugreek seeds
1 tablespoon fennel seeds

Soak the maize, wheat, and chickpeas or soybeans overnight. Drain the water and sun-dry them for a day or two. Soaking them prior to roasting makes *saatu* softer.

Roast the maize, wheat, and chickpeas separately in a thick-base pot or a *haandi* (a traditional clay pot with a narrow neck used for roasting grains and legumes) until they crack. Their colour will change and will start to pop as their skins or outer layer breaks.

Cool them down and mix them together. Grind them into flour using a large mortar and pestle or an electric grinder.

In a small pan, heat 5–6 tablespoons of ghee, and then fry the fenugreek and fennel seeds until they turn light brown. Strain out the seeds and pour melted ghee over the *saatu.*

Grind the fried fenugreek and fennel seeds into a powder and add it to the *saatu.* Then add the sugar. Mix them together by rubbing them lightly by hand. *Saatu* can be stored in airtight containers for several months. It can be

eaten simply as a porridge by adding hot milk or hot water. To make it more flavourful and nutritious, one can add a variety of fruits, berries, nuts, and honey. I prefer *saatu* with a pinch of salt to bring out and balance the flavours.

MASYAURA

Dried lentil nuggets

Masyaura are sun-dried lentil nuggets or balls commonly made from black lentils *(kalo maas)* and young taro or colocasia stems and leaves *(karkalo)*. Although there is no historic record on when and how the culture of making *masyaura* developed, it is likely one of the oldest Nepali preserved foods, given that both black lentils and taro are indigenous to the region and have been cultivated since ancient times.

The practice of making *masyaura* is common in many Nepali communities. As fresh vegetables were hard to find all year round in the past, *masyaura* was a nutritious alternative. Making *masyaura* is rather straight-forward. It only has two ingredients: lentils and greens. Black lentils and taro leaves are the traditional, most commonly used ingredients, but people nowadays also use gram flour, spring onions, garlic chives, and potatoes. Some Khas communities in the far-west make *masyaura* from horse gram and taro tuber. *Masyaura* has a unique flavour developed from the slight fermentation and sun-drying.

2 cups black lentils
A few stalks of young taro stems and/or leaves

Wash the young taro stems and/or leaves and leave them under sunlight for about half a day to wither. Soak the black lentils overnight.

Next morning, remove the black outer layer of the lentils by rubbing the soaked lentils with hands and washing them several times. It's not necessary to remove the layers completely. Drain the water, grind the lentils to make a paste, and place in a large bowl. Finely chop the young taro stems and/or leaves, and add to the lentil paste. Mix them together, cover the bowl, and leave for a couple of hours. This helps them mix well and also allows time for slight fermentation. Fermentation imparts a unique flavour to the dish.

Make small balls or nuggets using the hands and place them in a large tray or a *supo/mandro* (traditional bamboo mats used for drying lentils and other food items). Moisten the hands with water while making the nuggets to prevent the paste from sticking. These nuggets should be placed on the tray without touching each other.

Place the *masyaura* under direct sunlight for drying. They take about 3–4 days to dry completely, or more if the days are cloudy. They will also ferment slightly during the drying process. Keep them indoors during the night to speed up the drying process. Once they are completely dry, they will come off the tray. Keep them in an airtight container to store them for several months.

PINDALU MASYAURAKO JHOL

Taro and lentil nugget curry or soup

When fresh vegetables were difficult to find during the winter and dry seasons, *masyaura* (dried lentil nuggets) and *pindalu* (taro) were used as alterntatives to make curry or soup. No other ingredient pairs well with *masyaura* than taro. The soup is commonly consumed in the foothills and also in the plains.

1 large-size taro
A handful of *masyaura*
1 small-size radish, optional
2–3 tomatoes
1 medium-sized onion
1 teaspoon cumin seeds
1 teaspoon coriander seeds
1–2 red chillies
3–4 garlic cloves
1 thumb-sized ginger
1 teaspoon turmeric powder
1 tablespoon ghee
2–3 tablespoons vegetable oil
1 lime/lemon
Salt as per taste
Fresh coriander leaves or dill, for garnishing

*serves 3–4 people

First make a curry paste by grinding together the garlic cloves, ginger, chillies, and coriander and cumin seeds with a tablespoon of water.

Remove the skin of the taro. Cut the taro into bite-sized pieces. Making the surface of the taro pieces uneven helps them to cook faster: for this, cut the taro almost halfway through and push the knife outward to crack it into small pieces.

Heat a tablespoon of ghee in a cooking pot over medium heat. When the oil is hot, fry the *masyaura* and stir them constantly until brown. This should take about 2 minutes. Transfer the fried *masyaura* to a bowl.

In the same pot, add two tablespoons of vegetable oil and fry the fenugreek seeds. Then add the finely sliced onions and cook until light brown. Add the turmeric powder and then the curry paste, and fry until light brown. Add the diced tomatoes, the fried *masyaura,* and salt. Cook for about 3–4 minutes, or until the tomatoes melt, and add about 4 cups of water.

As the water starts boiling, add the taro pieces (and some sliced radish if preferred). Put the lid on and cook for around 15–20 minutes, or until the taro is properly cooked. Squeeze a tablespoon of lime juice into the soup to add flavour and also to remove the taro skin's acrid property.

Turn off the heat and garnish the with fresh coriander leaves or dill. Serve hot as a side dish with rice.

Note: Make sure hands are dry while handling taro and that the taro is properly cooked to avoid or eliminate its acrid property. Cooking with lemon juice helps eliminate the irritating nature of oxalates found in the taro.

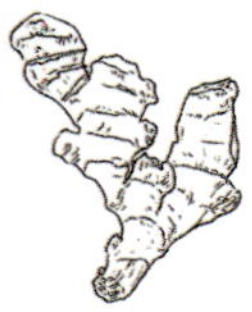

PHANDOKO JHOL

Roasted soybean flour soup

Phando is prepared by roasting legumes such as soybeans and chickpeas, and then grinding them into fine flour. It can be stored for several months, and made into a quick, simple, and nutritious soup. It usually works as a substitute for daal when one is in a hurry. The Kirat, Magar, Thakali, and other hilly communities also have a culture of making *phando*.

3–4 tablespoons *phando*
1 medium-sized onion
2–3 garlic cloves
1–2 green chillies
½ teaspoon cumin seeds
½ teaspoon fenugreek seeds
½ teaspoon turmeric powder
1–2 tablespoons vegetable oil or *ghee*
Fresh coriander leaves, for garnishing
Salt as per taste

*serves 3–4 people

Finely slice the onion and garlic cloves, and cut the green chillies in half.

To make *phando* soup, heat 2–3 tablespoons of vegetable oil or ghee in a cooking pot over medium heat. When the oil is hot enough, add the cumin and fenugreek seeds. After the seeds start to pop, add the onion, garlic, and green chillies, and fry until they become soft and aromatic. Add the turmeric powder and then the *phando*. Stir the mixture for half a minute and add 3–4 cups of water. Add the salt and red chilli powder according to taste. Bring to a boil and let it simmer for 4–5 minutes. Turn off the heat and garnish the soup with the fresh coriander leaves. *Phando* is usually eaten as a substitute for daal.

GUNDRUK

Fermented greens

Making *gundruk* (sun-dried fermented greens) is probably one of the oldest food preservation traditions in Nepal. There is no known historical evidence on when and how the culture of making *gundruk* started. But according to folklore, it was accidentally discovered by farmers in around the 12th century when they hid their grains and vegetables underground to save them from invaders. During the period, Khas and Magar kings from the west used to regularly attack the Kathmandu Valley. When the farmers dug out their produce, the greens had fermented and they loved the sour fermented flavour. The radishes had fermented into *sinki* and newly harvested rice grains had turned into light reddish, fermented *hakuwa* rice.

According to another story, *gundruk* was discovered by the soldiers when the greens they were carrying for several days as a part of their food supply on the way to the battlefield fermented.

Whatever the story, it is evident that *gundruk* originated in Nepal's hilly regions and later spread to other parts. Perceived as an unappealing food in the past, it is now a much-loved delicacy that evokes a sense of nostalgia.

Gundruk is considered quintessential Nepali food. Many ethnic communities have traditions of making *gundruk*. Typically, broadleaf mustard greens and radish greens are used to make *gundruk*. When there is a surplus of these greens, especially leftover hardy leaves at the end of the season, they are fermented and then sun-dried for preservation. Fermentation also develops *gundruk's* unique flavour. In earlier days, withered greens were beaten in large stone or wooden mortars and then compacted into a narrow-neck clay pot. These pots were then put in an underground pit and left for a week or more for fermenting. *Gundruk* provided essential nutrients during the dry season when fresh vegetables were difficult to find. It is commonly made into an achaar or a soup, often prepared together with roasted soybeans.

Broadleaf mustard greens

Thoroughly wash the broadleaf mustard greens to remove any dirt. Leave the leaves under direct sunlight for half a day to allow them to wither.

Smash the withered greens using a large mortar and pestle, or simply smash them using a rolling pin.

Compress the smashed greens in a jar (traditionally in a clay pot) up to the neck. Pour a few tablespoons of warm water, close the jar and put it outdoors for at least 10–15 days to ferment. Do not use metal jars for fermenting.

Once a strong acidic aroma starts to rise, take the greens out, spread them on a large mat or tray, and dry them under sunlight for at least 2–3 days. Sun-drying imparts extra flavour to the *gundruk* and helps to preserve it for several months to a year.

GWARCHA

Lentil soup with millet dumplings

Gwarcha is a black lentil soup or daal with millet flour dumplings prepared especially during the winter season. The dish reminds me of my childhood. I grew up in a hilly area where millet is grown abundantly and is one of the staple crops. My mother used to make *gwarcha* every now and then, but it is rarely prepared nowadays. In the Kathmandu Valley, whole wheat flour is used instead of millet flour to make dumplings for *gwarcha*.

1 cup millet flour
1 cup black lentil, split
4–5 garlic cloves
1 thumb-sized ginger
1–2 dry red chillies
1 teaspoon cumin seeds
1 teaspoon coriander seeds
1 teaspoon turmeric powder
1–2 tablespoons ghee/butter
Fresh coriander leaves, for garnishing
Salt as per taste

*serves 3–4 people

Grind together the ginger, garlic, red chillies, and cumin and coriander seeds to make a spice paste.

Take a cup of millet flour in a large bowl. Slowly pour about half a cup of water over the flour and mix them together to form dough. Leave aside to rest.

Wash the split black lentils to remove any impurities and place in a pressure cooker with about three cups of water. Add the spice paste, salt, and turmeric powder to the pressure cooker. Put the lid on, turn the heat to medium and cook for about 15–20 minutes or for 4–5 whistles. Turn off the heat and let the steam release by itself.

Take the lid off the pressure cooker after all the steam releases and lightly mash the cooked lentils. This helps to thicken the daal. Add about three cups of water, preferably hot, and simmer over medium heat. When the soup/daal starts boiling, make small round dumplings from the dough, and drop them into the soup. Cook for another 12–15 minutes with an occasional stir. Add 1–2 tablespoons of ghee for additional flavour and stir the mixture. Turn off the heat and garnish with the fresh coriander leaves.

AALU CAULI TARKARI

Potato and cauliflower curry

A Nepali meal isn't complete without a curry. Hundreds of varieties of seasonal vegetables, including wild and preserved ones, are used to make curries. Although the potato and cauliflower are not indigenous and were introduced to Nepal not too long ago, they are now the most consumed vegetables. Cauliflower was first introduced to Nepal as an ornamental plant and is now widely grown and consumed across the country. Every household has its own variation in making curries, including the choice of spices. Depending on the vegetables and the preference, the cooking time, process, and use of spices vary. The curry recipe below is a typical one and can be used for almost any type of vegetable.

3–4 medium-sized potatoes
½ kg cauliflower
2–3 medium-sized tomatoes
1 medium-sized onion
3–4 garlic cloves
1 thumb-sized ginger
1 teaspoon cumin powder
1 teaspoon coriander powder
1 teaspoon red chilli powder
1 teaspoon turmeric powder
1 teaspoon fenugreek seeds
Salt as per taste
2–3 tablespoons vegetable oil

*serves 3–4 people

Wash the potatoes properly or peel off their skins. Cut into bite-sized pieces. Also cut the cauliflower into bite-sized florets. Instead of directly cooking the cauliflower, one can also deep-fry the florets prior to making curry, as done in Nepal's southern plains.

Make a garlic and ginger paste. Finely slice the onion and chop the tomatoes.

Heat 2–3 tablespoons of vegetable oil in a cooking pan over medium heat. When the oil is hot enough, add the fenugreek seeds. After the seeds start popping, add the ginger and garlic paste, and onion slices. When the onion is soft and light brown, add the turmeric powder and the potatoes. Fry for a couple of minutes and add cauliflower. Cook them together for around 6–8 minutes stirring occasionally.

Add the cumin, coriander and red chilli powder, and salt. Stir and cook for about 3–4 minutes. Then add the chopped tomatoes, and cook for about 12–15 minutes with the lid on, stirring occasionally. Add some water in between if required to prevent the curry from burning. When the tomatoes melt completely and the potatoes are well cooked, the curry is ready.

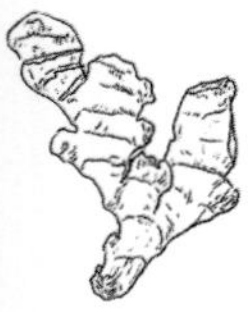

TAMAKO TARKARI

Stir-fried fresh bamboo shoots

Bamboo shoots (*tama*), available during the early monsoon season, are delicious to eat. When there are abundant bamboo shoots to consume fresh, they are preserved by fermentation. Fresh bamboo shoots are boiled to reduce their bitterness and then stir-fried to make a curry. They have a crunchy texture and add freshness to the curry.

½ kg fresh bamboo shoot
2 medium-sized potatoes
1 small onion
2–3 garlic cloves
1 thumb-sized ginger
2–3 medium-sized tomatoes
1–2 green chillies
1 teaspoon fenugreek seeds
1 teaspoon cumin seeds
1 teaspoon turmeric powder
1 tablespoon mustard seeds, coarsely crushed
1 teaspoon cumin powder
1 teaspoon coriander powder
1 teaspoon red chilli powder
2–3 tablespoons mustard oil
Salt as per taste

*serves 3–4 people

Remove the outer layers of the bamboo shoot until the soft compact white flesh appears. Cut into half or quarters if they have large girths, and then cut into thin slices.

Wash the bamboo slices and boil them in water in a pot for about 12–15 minutes. This will make the shoots tender and reduce their bitterness as well. Drain the water and immerse the shoots in cold water.

Peel the potatoes and cut them into thin slices. Finely slice the onion, ginger, garlic, and tomatoes, and halve green chillies.

Heat 2–3 tablespoons of mustard oil in a pan, and fry the fenugreek and cumin seeds. Immediately after the seeds start popping, add the finely sliced onion, minced ginger and garlic, and halved green chillies. Fry them for about a minute or until they become soft, aromatic, and light-brown. Then add the turmeric powder. Immediately add the potato slices and stir-fry them for about 2–3 minutes. Add the boiled bamboo shoots slices and stir-fry them for about 4–5 minutes. Sprinkle the salt and coarsely ground mustard seeds. Add the cumin, coriander, and red chilli powder, and the tomatoes. Stir and cook for 3–4 minutes with the lid on or until the tomatoes melt. Squeeze half a lime or lemon, stir and cook for another 3–4 minutes with the lid on. Add a few tablespoons of water in between if necessary.

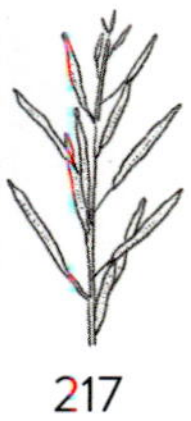

NIUROKO TARKARI

Sauteed fiddlehead fern

Fiddlehead fern (*niuro* or *niguro*) is one of the common wild vegetables consumed across Nepal. It is harvested year-round in the southern plains and available only during the monsoon season in the hilly and mountainous regions. I remember, when young, we used to go to the nearby forest to collect fiddlehead fern during the weekends and holidays. *Kali niuro*, a variety of the fern with a dark brown stalk, was favoured over others as it was perceived to be rare and more delicious. When in season, fiddlehead fern is a common vegetable in the countryside and a prized delicacy in the urban areas.

½ kg or a big handful of fiddlehead fern
2–3 garlic cloves
1–2 red chillies, fresh or dried
1 teaspoon fenugreek seeds
1 teaspoon mustard seeds
½ teaspoon turmeric powder
2–3 tablespoons sesame seeds
½ teaspoon *timmur*
1 teaspoon cumin and coriander powder mix
1 tablespoon lemon or lime juice
2–3 tomatoes, optional
2 tablespoons vegetable oil, or preferably *ghee*
Salt as per taste

*serves 3–4 people

Remove the bottom hardy end of the fiddlehead fern stalks and snap the tender fronds into about two-inch-long pieces. If the fronds are thick, split them into half using a knife. Wash the fiddlehead fern thoroughly with clean water to remove hairs.

Boil the fronds in water with a teaspoon of salt and lemon juice for about 10–12 minutes or until they becomes tender. Then drain the water.

Lightly roast the sesame seeds in a pan, let them cool, and grind into coarse grounds.

In a pan, heat two tablespoons of vegetable oil or ghee over medium heat. When the oil is hot enough, add the fenugreek and mustard seeds. After the seeds start popping, fry the whole red chillies, and finely sliced or minced garlic. When the garlic turns light brown, add the turmeric powder and then the fiddlehead fern. Sauté for about 8–10 minutes over medium heat, stirring occasionally.

Add the cumin and coriander powder, salt, and tomatoes (optional). Add the roasted sesame seed and *timmur* grounds. Give everything a stir and sauté for another 4–6 minutes. The crunchy sautéed fiddlehead fern is ready.

TARULKO TARKARI

Yam curry

Yam (*tarul*) is a wild tuber that's widely consumed in Nepal. A few varieties are also grown in the fields. Indigenous to the South Asian region, it was a sustenance food for hilly communities during winter in the early days when other vegetables were not available. I still remember going with my father to the forest to forage for wild yam. Digging out the yam is a time-consuming, labour-intensive process as it can easily grow over a metre in length below the ground. Boiled yam is an essential dish during the Maghe Sakranti festival. It is also consumed as a curry.

½ kg yam
3–4 potatoes, optional
1 medium-sized onion
2–3 tomatoes, optional
½ teaspoon fenugreek seeds
1 teaspoon cumin seeds
1 teaspoon coriander seeds
1–2 red chillies
3–4 garlic cloves
½ inch piece ginger
1 teaspoon turmeric powder
2–3 tablespoons vegetable oil

*serves 3–4 people

First, make a curry paste by grinding together the cumin and coriander seeds, garlic cloves, ginger, and dry red chillies with a tablespoon of water in a *silauto* (traditional stone-made mortar and pestle) or an electric grinder.

Wash the yam and potatoes, and remove their skins. Cut them into bite-sized pieces. Finely slice the onion.

In a pan, heat 2–3 tablespoons of vegetable oil over medium heat. When the oil is hot enough, fry the fenugreek seeds and then the onion. When the onion becomes soft and light brown, add the turmeric powder. Then immediately add the yam and potatoes, and stir-fry for 4–5 minutes. Add the salt and the curry paste, and cook for another 4–5 minutes. Add the tomatoes and cook for a few more minutes until they melt. Add about two cups of water and slow-cook for about 15–20 minutes or until the yam and potatoes are well cooked. Turn off the heat and the yam curry is ready.

RUKH KATAHARKO TARKARI

Jackfruit curry

Jackfruit *(rukh katahar)* is abundant in the plains and hills, available from around April to July. It can be eaten as a vegetable when young and as a fruit when ripe. The young ones are usually cooked as curry. Seeds from the ripe fruit can also be roasted or cooked into a curry. When ripe, jackfruit develops a sweetness with a distinctive fruity aroma. The fruit can grow as big as 10–15 kilograms. Easily grown in less fertile and dry soil, this humble fruit could help address the food insecurity exacerbated by climate change and pest infections.

1 kg young jackfruit
1 small onion
2–3 potatoes
2–3 tomatoes, optional
4–5 garlic cloves
2-inch-long or a large thumb-sized ginger
½ teaspoon fenugreek seeds
½ teaspoon mustard seeds
1 teaspoon cumin seeds
1 teaspoon coriander seeds
2–3 dry red chillies
1 teaspoon turmeric powder
3–4 tablespoons vegetable oil
Salt as per taste

*serves 4–5 people

The young jackfruit has sticky sap, so oil your hands, knife, and chopping board before cutting. Cut the two ends of the jackfruit and let the sap ooze out for a few minutes. Remove the thick skin of the jackfruit, cut the flesh into quarters and again, cut each piece into half to make them more manageable to cut into bite-sized chunks. Remove the inner dense white core. Steam or boil the jackfruit for about 15 minutes for its fibrous flesh to tenderise.

Meanwhile, wash and peel the potatoes and cut them into bite-sized cubes. When the steamed jackfruit cools, drain the water, and cut the jackfruit into bite-sized chunks.

Make a curry paste by grinding together the cumin and coriander seeds, garlic cloves, ginger, and dry red chillies. Finely slice the onion and tomatoes.

Heat 3–4 tablespoons of vegetable oil in a pan over medium heat. When the oil is hot enough, fry the fenugreek and mustard seeds. Then add the onion slices and turmeric powder, and fry until the onion slices become soft and light brown. Add the potatoes and cook for 2–3 minutes. Then add steamed jackfruit chunks and cook for about 4–5 minutes, stirring occasionally. Add the salt and curry paste, and cook for another 4–5 minutes. Add the tomatoes and cook for a few minutes until they melt. Add about a cup of water and cook the curry for about 15 minutes or until the potatoes and jackfruit are perfectly cooked.

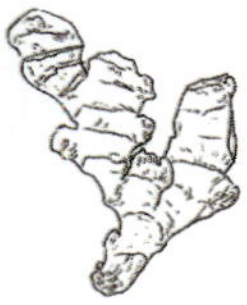

AJIKO RUKH KATAHARKO TARKARI

Grandmother's jackfruit curry

This jackfruit curry recipe from my grandmother (*aji*), who passed away a few years before I was born, was handed down to me by my mother. I tried her recipe based on my mother's recollection. According to her, grandmother used to marinate the jackfruit in yoghurt, spices, and salt, and then slow-cook it in a *kasaundi* for about an hour. Grandmother probably learned this recipe when she travelled to India. Yoghurt tenderises the jackfruit and imparts a creamy-sour flavour to the curry.

1 kg young jackfruit
½ cup yoghurt
4–5 garlic cloves
1 large thumb-sized ginger
½ teaspoon fenugreek seeds
½ teaspoon mustard seeds
1 teaspoon cumin seeds
1 teaspoon coriander seeds
2–3 dry red chillies
1 teaspoon turmeric powder
2–3 tablespoons mustard oil, or vegetable oil
Salt as per taste

*serves 4–5 people

Remove the skin and the central white core of a young jackfruit.

Cut the jackfruit into bite-sized pieces and place in a bowl. Add the yoghurt, salt, and turmeric powder to the bowl. Grind the garlic, ginger, cumin and coriander seeds, and dry red chillies together to make a paste. Add the paste to the jackfruit and yoghurt mixture, and mix them well with a ladle or by hand. Leave the mixture to marinate for at least 30 minutes, which also helps tenderise the jackfruit.

In a *kasaundi*, heat 2–3 tablespoons of mustard or vegetable oil. Fry the fenugreek and mustard seeds in the oil. When the seeds start popping, add the marinated jackfruit to the pot. Give it a stir and let it cook over medium heat for about 25–30 minutes with the lid on. Use a steel plate as a lid and put some water on the plate; this will help condense the steam as it rises and cook the curry in its own moisture. Add some water in between if required and stir occasionally to avoid burning. When the jackfruit becomes tender and cooked, turn off the heat, and the curry is ready.

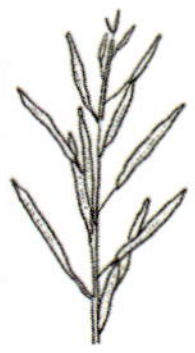

KARELA BHEDARI TARKARI

Bitter gourd and ladies' finger curry

Bitter gourd *(karela)* is one of my favourite vegetables. Once one is used to its bitterness, it can be delectable. A variety of dishes: fried, curry, fermented pickle, achaar/salad, and soup is prepared from bitter gourd. Bitter gourd and ladies' finger *(bhedari/chiple bhindi)* are often cooked together as a curry, and are popular in the Nepali kitchen.

300 gm bitter gourds
300 gm ladies' fingers
1 small onion
1–2 green chillies
3–4 medium size tomatoes
3–4 garlic cloves
1 small thumb-sized ginger
½ teaspoon fenugreek seeds
½ teaspoon cumin seeds
½ teaspoon mustard seeds
1 teaspoon cumin and coriander powder mix
½ teaspoon red chilli powder
½ teaspoon turmeric powder
1 lemon
Salt as per taste
1 cup vegetable oil, for frying

*serves 3–4 people

Wash the bitter gourds and ladies' fingers, remove the tips, and cut them into one-inch-long fingers.

In a pan, heat a cup of vegetable oil over medium heat. When the oil is hot enough, fry a handful of the chopped bitter gourds and ladies' fingers in batches until light brown. Each batch will take about 6–8 minutes of frying. Take the fried bitter gourds and ladies' fingers out of the pan using a slotted spoon.

When the frying is done, scoop out the remaining oil, leaving just a tablespoon in the pan. Fry the fenugreek, cumin, and mustard seeds. Then add the finely sliced onion, minced garlic and ginger, and green chillies (cut into halves). When the spices become light brown and aromatic, add the turmeric powder. Then add the tomatoes, fried bitter gourds and ladies' fingers, salt, and cumin, coriander, and red chilli powder. Cook for about 8–10 minutes over medium heat, stirring occasionally, until the tomatoes melt. Squeeze a lemon, stir, and turn off the heat.

TAREKO KARELA

Crispy deep-fried bitter gourd

The dish is prepared by deep-frying bitter gourds and has a crispy texture. The frying significantly reduces the gourd's bitterness. It is generally eaten as a side dish with *daal-bhat-tarkari.*

4–5 medium-sized bitter gourds
3–4 garlic cloves
½ teaspoon cumin and coriander powder mix
½ teaspoon red chilli powder
1 lemon
Salt as per taste
1 cup vegetable oil, for frying

*serves 3–4 people

Wash the bitter gourds and cut them into thin round slices.

In a pan, heat a cup of vegetable oil over medium heat. When the oil is hot enough, fry the bitter gourd slices in small batches, along with the smashed garlic. Take out the fried bitter gourd slices and garlic from the pan using a slotted spoon and transfer them to a bowl. Sprinkle some salt, and cumin, coriander, and red chilli powder over the bitter gourd. Squeeze a lemon and mix them well together. The crispy fried bitter gourd is ready.

GAVAKO TARKARI

Taro leaf curry

Indigenous to South Asia, taro is possibly one of the oldest cultivated vegetables in the region. Before the potato was introduced to the region, the taro was cultivated extensively and consumed on a regular basis as a variety of dishes. All parts of the taro plant are consumed as vegetables. The tuber of the plant is called *pindalu* and the young leaf is called *gava* or *karkaloko paat* in the Nepali language. Taro is a seasonal plant and is available from September to December. The calcium oxalates in the taro plant impart an acrid taste, so it should be well-cooked. Lemon juice or vinegar also helps remove its acridity.

A wide variety of dishes are prepared from the leaves, stems, and tubers of the taro plant. Tubers are usually cooked as a curry or sometimes simply boiled and eaten with a salt-chilli paste. Tubers can be stored for several months on their own, but can also be grated and sun-dried to make *pindaluko bhujuri,* which is later consumed by turning it into an achaar.

Taro leaves and stems are simply boiled and flavoured with tempered spices, salt, and lemon juice. When there is an abundance of taro leaves, my mother steams and sun-dries them for preservation. Later, they are cooked as a curry with potatoes. Stems can also be made into achaar and preserved by sun-drying. A popular traditional food *masyaura* is prepared from finely chopped leaves and stems with a lentil paste mixture. The leaves are like any other green vegetables, with a subtle flavour that tastes delicious if cooked well. The best way to eat this taro leaf curry is by smashing fresh green chillies and squeezing some lemon juice into it.

10–12 young taro leaves
3–4 garlic cloves
½ thumb-sized ginger
1 teaspoon fenugreek seeds
1 teaspoon mustard seeds
1 teaspoon turmeric powder
1 teaspoon cumin and coriander powder mix
2 lemons/limes
A few green chillies
1–2 tablespoons mustard oil
Salt as per taste

*serves 3–4 people

Put aside the fresh taro leaves for a day to let them wither slightly.

Roll the withered taro leaves tightly and make a knot. It is easier to roll the leaves if they are slightly withered. Forming a knot helps it cook well, and they hold together when cooked.

Put the taro leaf knots in a pot and add about a cup of water. Add the salt, two smashed garlic cloves, and smashed ginger. Boil for around 20 minutes with the lid on over medium heat. Press the leaves with a spatula to check if they are cooked; they will break easily if cooked. If not, add some hot water and cook further. Turn off the heat when the leaves are perfectly cooked and squeeze some lemon juice over them.

To temper the spices, heat a small pan and pour about 1–2 tablespoons of mustard oil. Add the fenugreek and mustard seeds, and the finely sliced garlic. Once the seeds start popping, add the cumin, coriander, and turmeric powder. Turn off the heat and pour the mixture over the taro leaf curry.

Stir the curry well, and serve with a slice of lemon and fresh green chilli.

RAYO SAAG

Sautéed broadleaf mustard greens

Broadleaf mustard greens are widely grown and consumed in Nepal. The young leaves are tender and have a mustardy flavour. Sautéed broadleaf mustard greens (or other seasonal greens) are a common side dish in the *daal-bhat-tarkari* staple. When there is an abundant amount of broadleaf mustard greens, they are fermented and dried to make *gundruk*.

A large handful of broadleaf mustard greens
2–3 garlic cloves
1–2 dry red chillies
½ teaspoon fenugreek seeds
½ teaspoon mustard seeds
½ teaspoon cumin seeds
½ teaspoon turmeric powder
2 tablespoons ghee or mustard oil
Salt as per taste

*serves 3–4 people

Wash the greens under running water and cut them into one-inch-long chunks.

Heat about two tablespoons of mustard oil or ghee in a pan. Then add fenugreek, cumin, and mustard seeds. When the seeds start to pop, fry red chillies and finely sliced garlic cloves until light brown. Add turmeric powder and chopped greens immediately. Sauté for about 6–8 minutes with an occasional stir and sprinkle some salt in between. Use as little salt as possible, and avoid overcooking as the greens will develop a bitter taste and lose their crunchy texture.

PHARSIKO MUNTAKO TARKARI

Sautéed young pumpkin shoots

During the monsoon season, young pumpkin shoots *(pharsiko munta)* are widely available and consumed as a vegetable. Pumpkins are usually planted with maize. The pumpkin plant grows wildly and produces lots of shoots. Pumpkin flowers are also consumed as a vegetable; it was a favourite of my maternal grandfather. The shoots have a crunchy texture and taste delicious, especially when stir-fried in ghee.

A big handful of young pumpkin shoots
2–3 garlic cloves
A half thumb-sized ginger
1–2 dry red chillies
½ teaspoon fenugreek seeds
½ teaspoon mustard seeds
½ teaspoon cumin seeds
½ teaspoon turmeric powder
1 teaspoon cumin and coriander powder mix
2–3 tablespoons *ghee*, or use butter/vegetable oil
Salt as per taste

*serves 3–4 people

The part closer to the tip of the shoots is tender. Remove the part at the other end that's not as tender. Also, remove the outer thin hairy layer by snapping the end and pulling the layers towards the tip. Then snap the shoots into about 1 ½-inch-long pieces. Wash them with clean water and drain properly.

Heat about 2–3 tablespoons of ghee in a pan. Add the fenugreek, cumin, and mustard seeds, dry red chillies, and minced ginger and garlic. When the ginger and garlic start to turn light brown, add the turmeric, cumin, and coriander powder, and then the young pumpkin shoots. Sauté for about 8–10 minutes over medium-high heat, or until the shoots become tender.

Stir occasionally. Sprinkle salt in between. Avoid overcooking.

SIPLIGANKO TARKARI

Sautéed wild bitter greens

Young tender leaves of *sipligan* or *siprigan* (*Crateva unilocularis*) tree are consumed as vegetables. These seasonal young leaves sprout each year in the spring (March–May). This mid-sized tree is found in the foothills and mid-hills. The young leaves have a strong bitter taste, but the bitterness is tempered during the cooking process. Soaking the greens overnight also reduces the bitterness. It is generally consumed by stir-frying or making into an achaar. My favourite way is to boil the greens with lime juice, and then sauté them with sesame seed grounds and spices. The leaves can also be preserved by blanching them first and then letting them ferment in a jar, which lends them a sour flavour and tempers the bitterness. *Sipligan* is more of an acquired taste. My mother loves it.

½ kg *sipligan*
3–4 garlic cloves
1–2 dry red chillies
½ teaspoon fenugreek seeds
½ teaspoon mustard seeds
½ teaspoon turmeric powder
½ teaspoon cumin and coriander powder mix
2–3 tablespoons sesame seeds
2–3 tablespoons mustard, or vegetable oil
1 teaspoon *chuk* (concentrated Nepali lemon juice) or 1 lime/lemon

*serves 3–4 people

Soak the young *sipligan* leaves overnight in water. Drain the water the next day and boil the leaves for about 15 minutes with a teaspoon of *chuk* or lemon juice until they become soft. Soaking the leaves overnight and boiling them helps temper their bitterness. After boiling, wash the leaves a couple of times with cold water.

In a small pan, lightly roast the sesame seeds. Let the seeds cool and grind them into a coarse powder.

In a pan, heat 2–3 tablespoons of mustard oil. Fry the dry red chillies, fenugreek and mustard seeds, and finely chopped garlic. Add some turmeric, cumin and coriander powder, and then add the *sipligan* leaves. Sprinkle salt and sauté for 3–4 minutes. Add the roasted sesame seeds grounds, squeeze a lime, and pour in a few tablespoons of water. Cook for another couple of minutes and the sautéed *sipligan* is ready.

KHASIKO MASU

Goat meat curry

Goat meat (colloquially called mutton in South Asia) is among the most commonly consumed meat among Nepalis. Customarily, it is an occasional delicacy consumed during major celebrations and festivals, especially Dashain. In many Hindu households, a male goat is sacrificed to the gods during festivals. The meat is cooked into various delicacies: lean meat is dry cooked or made into a curry, bone-in meat is made into a soup, offal is cooked as *bhutuwa*, and surplus meat is smoke-dried to make *sukuti*. Dashain, for me, is still partly about the aroma and flavour of deliciously cooked goat meat.

Bone-in and skin-on goat meat is used to make a curry, instead of just boneless meat. Bone marrow and fat enhance the flavour of the dish. Goat meat is flavoursome in itself, so it doesn't require much effort and lots of spices to enhance its flavour. However, this recipe uses a large variety of spices that won't overpower the flavour of the meat; it's one of my favourite recipes.

1 kg bone-in goat meat, cut into bite-sized pieces
1 medium-sized red onion, finely sliced
2–3 medium-sized tomatoes
1 tablespoon minced garlic
1 tablespoon minced ginger
3–4 cloves
3–4 green cardamom
1–2 black cardamom
1 cinnamon stick
2–3 bay leaves *(tejpata)*
1 teaspoon fenugreek seeds
1 tablespoon cumin and coriander powder
1 tablespoon *garam masala*, optional
1 teaspoon red chilli powder
1 teaspoon turmeric powder
2–3 tablespoons vegetable oil
Salt as per taste
Fresh coriander leaves, for garnishing

*Serves 4–5 people

Heat 3–4 tablespoons of vegetable oil in a pressure cooker or *kasaundi* over medium heat. If using an ordinary pot, the meat will take longer to cook. Fry the cloves, green cardamom, black cardamom, cinnamon, bay leaves, and then the fenugreek seeds for around 15–20 seconds or until they become aromatic.

Add the finely chopped red onion and minced ginger and garlic. Fry them until they are soft and turn light brown. Then add the turmeric powder. Add the goat meat and cook for around 10–12 minutes or until the meat starts to turn brown. Stir occasionally. Add the salt and cumin, coriander, and red chilli powder. Cook for another 3–4 minutes, stirring occasionally. Add the diced tomatoes, and cook for another 4–5 minutes or until the tomatoes melt.

Add the *garam masala* (optional), stir the curry, and pour about one and a half cups of water. Put the lid on the pressure cooker and cook for around 15–20 minutes (or about 2–3 whistles) over low heat. If using a regular pot, cook the curry for around 30–40 minutes over low heat with the lid on. Turn off the heat and let the cooker cool. Don't take the lid off until steam inside the pressure cooker releases completely.

Add about a cup of water, bring to a boil, and cook further for about five minutes. Turn off the heat and garnish the goat meat curry with the fresh coriander leaves.

KHASIKO MASU RA KWANTIKO JHOL

Goat meat and sprouted mixed beans soup

Kwanti, prepared with nine varieties of sprouted beans or legumes, is a cultural food of the Newa community. It is cooked especially during Kwanti Punhi or Janai Purnima, an important festival for both the Newa and Khas communities. The Newas sometimes cook *kwanti* with buffalo meat. Some non-Newas living in Kathmandu have adapted the Newa recipe using goat meat. *Kwanti* soup becomes even more delicious when cooked with bone-in meat. This soup cooked with goat meat is one of my favourites, and I often make it during the festival.

1 ½ cups of *kwanti* (sprouted mixed beans)
½ kg mutton with bones and some fat, cut into bite-sized pieces
1 medium-sized red onion, finely sliced
2–3 medium-sized tomatoes , chopped
3–4 bay leaves
1 tablespoon minced garlic
1 tablespoon minced ginger
1 tablespoon cumin and coriander powder mix
1 teaspoon red chilli powder
1 teaspoon turmeric powder
1 teaspoon ajwain seeds *(jwano)*
1 teaspoon fenugreek seeds
Salt as per taste
3 tablespoons vegetable oil
Fresh coriander leaves

Marinating the meat
1 teaspoon cumin and coriander powder mix
½ teaspoon red chilli powder
1 teaspoon minced ginger and garlic
½ teaspoon black pepper
1 tablespoon vegetable oil
1 teaspoon salt

*Serves 4–5 people

To sprout the beans: soak the beans overnight in water. Drain the water and wrap them in a moist muslin cloth. Keep aside for 2–3 days to let them sprout. Sprinkle some water once or twice to keep them moist. Or one can simply make the soup from soaked beans instead of sprouted beans.

To marinate the meat: A few hours or at least 30 minutes before cooking, marinate the meat by mixing it with the minced garlic and ginger, cumin, coriander, and red chilli powder, black pepper, salt, and a tablespoon of vegetable oil. Put aside for marination.

Heat about three tablespoons of vegetable oil in a pressure cooker. When the oil is hot enough, fry the bay leaves and fenugreek and *ajwain* seeds. When the seeds start popping, add the finely sliced onion and minced ginger and garlic, and cook until light brown. Add the turmeric powder and the marinated meat immediately. Fry the meat for around 8–10 minutes or until light brown over medium heat.

Add the sprouted *kwanti*, tomatoes, cumin powder, coriander powder, red chilli powder, and salt. Stir well and cook for another 7–8 minutes.

Pour about two cups of water (preferably hot); put the lid on the pressure cooker and cook for 14–15 minutes over low heat or for around 3–4 whistles. Turn off the heat and let the steam release on its own.

Take the lid off once the steam is gone, turn the heat back on, and add about 4–5 cups of hot water (depending on the quantity of soup desired). Adjust salt if required. Boil for about 10 minutes over medium heat.

Garnish with the fresh coriander leaves, and serve the soup as a starter or with rice or roti.

KHASIKO BHUTUWA

Goat offal meat cooked with blood

Bhutuwa is a prized delicacy prepared especially during major festivals such as Dashain when animals are slaughtered at home. It is prepared by cooking blood and offal including tongue, cheek, and ear. Almost all Nepali communities make *bhutuwa*. This delicacy is especially cooked for the people involved in slaughtering and processing the meat. After the meat is processed, people sit together and eat *bhutuwa*. In many communities, it is enjoyed with alcoholic drinks.

1 kg goat offal, including fatty meat pieces
2 cups fresh goat blood
3–4 bay leaves
1 medium-sized onion, finely sliced
2–3 green chillies, finely sliced
1 tablespoon garlic paste
1 tablespoon ginger paste
1 tablespoon cumin and coriander powder mix
1 teaspoon turmeric powder
1 teaspoon red chilli powder, optional
2–3 tablespoons vegetable oil
Fresh coriander leaves, for garnishing
Salt as per taste

*Serves 4–5 people

First clean the offal and boil them in water with half a teaspoon of turmeric for about 15–20 minutes. Then cut them into bite-sized pieces, including the other organs and fatty meat.

Heat 2–3 tablespoons of vegetable oil in a large pan over medium heat. When the oil is hot, first add the fatty meat and fry it for 3–4 minutes to render the fat. Fry the bay leaves, finely sliced onions, chillies, and ginger and garlic paste until they turn light brown. Then add the turmeric powder. Add the offal pieces and fry them for about 15–20 minutes, stirring occasionally. Add the salt and cumin, coriander, and red chilli powder, and fry for another 4–5 minutes.

Add the fresh blood and stir. If the blood is coagulated, mash it by hand first. Cook for another 12–15 minutes while stirring occasionally. The *bhutuwa* is ready. Garnish with coriander leaves before serving. It can be eaten as a snack on its own or with beaten rice and alcohol.

BHUTEKO RANGOKO MASU

Stir-fried buffalo meat

Dashain or Mohani festival used to be all about going to *mamaghar* (maternal uncle's house) and enjoying buffalo meat (buff) cooked into a variety of dishes. I enjoyed eating meat roasted directly over the fire. In the Newa community, buffaloes are sacrificed during festivals; it's a big communal affair and the meat is distributed among the community.

Stir-fried buff, usually using lean meat, is a commonly prepared dish during festivals at home and *mamaghar.* It is eaten together with beaten rice and *selroti.* While bone-in meat is prepared into a soup. Buff pairs well with ginger, and is cooked with a generous amount of the root.

1 kg buffalo meat
1 medium-sized onion
1 tablespoon garlic paste
3–4 tablespoons ginger paste
1 tablespoon cumin and coriander powder mix
1 teaspoon red chilli powder
1 teaspoon turmeric powder
2–3 bay leaves
3–4 tablespoons vegetable oil
A few stalks of coriander leaves, for garnishing
Salt as per taste

*Serves 4–5 people

Cut the buffalo meat into bite-sized pieces.

Heat 3–4 tablespoons of vegetable oil in a large frying pan (preferably a cast-iron pan) over medium heat. Fry the bay leaves, finely chopped onions, and ginger and garlic paste. When they become soft and light brown, add the turmeric powder and then immediately the meat. Dial up the heat and fry it for about 12–15 minutes stirring occasionally. The meat will first release its juice and later start to caramelise.

Add the salt and cumin, coriander, and red chilli powder. Reduce the heat to medium, and cook for another 12–15 minutes with the lid on, stirring occasionally. Add a quarter cup of water in between. After the meat is cooked, turn off the heat, and garnish with the fresh coriander leaves. This tender stir-fried meat can be eaten on its own or with roti, rice, beaten rice, or puffed rice.

FARSI RA SUKUTIKO TARKARI

Pumpkin and smoke-dried meat curry

Surplus meat during the festivals, especially Dashain, is hung over firewood smoke to dry. This smoke-dried meat is known as *sukuti*, a beloved delicacy. Smoke-drying is a common method for preserving meat and also helps to intensify the meat's flavour.

I remember buff *sukuti* being prepared during Dashain at *mamaghar* to be cooked with yellow pumpkin during Tihar. Pumpkin and *sukuti* go well together, and the particular combination is also enjoyed by many other ethnic communities in the hills. The curry has a sweet taste from the pumpkin and a smoky flavour from the *sukuti*. When young, I wasn't really fond of yellow pumpkin curry because of its sweetness and would only eat the *sukuti*. But now, I love this curry.

150–200 gm buff *sukuti*
½ kg pumpkin
4–5 garlic cloves
1 thumb-sized ginger
1 teaspoon cumin seeds
1 teaspoon coriander seeds
2–3 red chillies
1 teaspoon fenugreek seeds
1 teaspoon mustard seeds
1 teaspoon turmeric powder
2–3 bay leaves (*tejpatta*)
2–3 tablespoons vegetable oil
1 lemon/lime
Salt as per taste

*Serves 3–4 people

First soak the *sukuti* in hot water for around 15–20 minutes to soften. Then drain the water and cut the soaked *sukuti* into bite-sized pieces.

Make a curry paste by grinding the garlic, ginger, cumin and coriander seeds, and red chillies together using a mortar and pestle or an electric grinder.

Remove the pumpkin's skin and seeds, and cut into bite-sized pieces.

Heat 2–3 tablespoons of vegetable oil in a cooking pan over medium heat. When the oil is about to smoke, fry the bay leaves, fenugreek and mustard seeds, and turmeric powder. Immediately add the *sukuti*, and fry for around 5-6 minutes. Then add the pumpkin and cook for another 4–5 minutes. Add the salt and the spice paste, and cook further for a couple of minutes.

Add about two cups of water, put the lid on, and cook for around 15–20 minutes until the pumpkin becomes soft. Gently smash the pumpkin with a spatula: this will thicken the gravy. Add a tablespoon of lemon or lime juice to balance the pumpkin's sweetness. Turn off the heat and the delicious pumpkin and *sukuti* curry is ready.

SEKUWA

Barbecued meat marinated with spices

Meat cooked or barbecued over a wood fire is called *sekuwa*. It is derived from the word *sekne*, which in the Nepali language means to cook over direct heat. *Sekuwa* has slowly become customary during gatherings with families and friends, and during festivals. It is often eaten together with puffed rice, beaten rice, and achaar. One can use any meat: pork, goat meat, buffalo meat, or chicken. Some people use a fair amount of spices to marinate the meat, but some prefer to keep the meat plain. Choose meat with some fat in it as it will impart a rich flavour to the dish.

1 kg boneless chicken, cut into medium-sized pieces
1 tablespoon garlic paste
1 tablespoon ginger paste
1 tablespoon cumin and coriander powder mix
1 teaspoon red chilli powder
1 teaspoon turmeric powder
½ teaspoon black pepper powder
2–3 tablespoons of vegetable oil
Salt as per taste

Garnishing
1 large red onion, finely sliced
1–2 lemons

*serves 3–4 people

First, marinate the chicken pieces by mixing all the spices, salt (to taste), and vegetable oil. Let it marinate for at least a couple of hours (better overnight in a refrigerator).

Skew the marinated meat in a metal or moist bamboo skewer. Prepare the wood fire for barbecuing. When enough charcoal forms, barbecue the meat, rotating the skewer occasionally until the meat is cooked. It will take around 12–15 minutes to cook, depending upon the intensity of the fire and the size of the meat. Serve hot with onion and lemon slices. It can also be served with *timmur* and tomato achaar.

MACHHAKO JHOL

Fish curry or soup

When young, summer holidays meant going swimming and fishing to the nearby river with friends. We used simple handmade traps and spears or our bare hands to catch fish. An easy way of making a trap was by taking a large bowl with some *jaand* (fermented rice or millet) and covering it with a cotton cloth with a small hole. The bowl was then submerged in the water. The *jaand* would attract fish into the trap.

These river fish make a delicious soup, which used to be an occasional treat at our home growing up.

Freshwater fish is also a key source of protein in Nepali diets. Rivers, streams, lakes, ponds, swamps, and irrigated paddy fields in the lowlands of the Tarai and mountains support a diverse variety of fishes. *Asala*, a Himalayan river trout, is a much sought-after variety of fish in the hilly areas, as is *rohu* in the plains. Some indigenous communities in Nepal traditionally depend on fishing for their livelihoods. For the Tharus, Maithils, and Newas, fish also has religious and cultural significance.

1 kg freshwater fish, gutted and cleaned
3–4 medium size tomatoes
1 medium-sized onion
2 fresh chillies
1 teaspoon mustard seeds
1 tablespoon cumin and coriander powder
1 teaspoon fenugreek seeds
6–8 garlic cloves
1 thumb-sized ginger
1–2 lime/lemon
Salt as per taste
3 tablespoons mustard oil
Fresh coriander leaves, for garnishing

*serves 3–4 people

Cut the cleaned fish into one-inch-thick pieces. If the fish are small, they can be cooked whole.

Finely slice the onion, chop the tomatoes, cut the green chillies into half, and make a ginger and garlic paste.

Heat about three tablespoons of mustard oil in a large pan. When the oil is hot, fry the fenugreek and mustard seeds. When the seeds start popping, add the sliced onion, halved green chillies, and garlic and ginger paste. Fry until they are soft and light brown. Add the turmeric powder and then the finely chopped tomatoes, and salt to taste. Cook the tomatoes for about 4–5 minutes, or until they melt completely. Add the cumin and coriander powder, give a good stir, and cook for another 6–8 minutes or until the oil and spices start separating.

Add about four cups of hot water and bring to a boil. Then add the fish pieces, pour some lemon juice, and give it a gentle stir. Cook over medium heat for around 14–15 minutes. Don't stir vigorously as it will break the flesh. Turn off the heat, give a gentle stir and garnish with the fresh coriander leaves. Let it rest for about five minutes before serving. The fish soup becomes more delicious the next day as the flesh soaks up all the flavours from the soup.

TAREKO SANO MACHHA

Deep-fried small fish

Deep-fried small fish are eaten as a snack and also as a *sitan* (light food eaten as an accompaniment with alcohol). Small fish are also preserved by smoke-drying, which is known as *sidhra*, a sought-after delicacy. Every household has its own recipe and blend of spices for deep-frying fish. Plain flour is commonly used nowadays instead of maize flour.

1 kg small fishes, gutted and cleaned
1 cup maize flour
1 teaspoon ginger paste
1 teaspoon garlic paste
1 teaspoon cumin and coriander powder
½ teaspoon red chilli powder, optional
½ teaspoon turmeric powder
½ litre vegetable oil, for frying
1–2 lemons
Salt as per taste

*serves 3–4 people

First prepare a thick batter in a bowl by mixing maize flour, all the spices, and salt with water.

Heat half a litre of vegetable oil in a deep frying pan over medium heat. When the oil is hot enough, dip the fish in the batter and fry them in the oil for about 3–4 minutes or until they turn light brown. Use a slotted spoon to take the fish out and drain off the excess oil. Fry the fish in batches, and don't overcrowd the pan. Serve with lemon slices and freshly ground roasted tomato achaar.

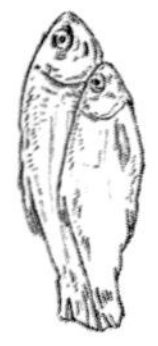

POLEKO RA BHUTEKO HARIYO MAKAI

Roasted and stir-fried fresh unripe maize

Maize is a relatively new crop in Nepal, but has become one of the staples of communities across Nepal. The history of maize in Nepal is obscure, but it is known to have been cultivated extensively in the hilly areas only by the mid-17th century. It is often cultivated intercropped with millet. Unripe maize, when its kernels are still sweet and in the milk stage, is also consumed. The freshly harvested unripe maize on the cob (*hariyo makai*) is roasted, boiled, or its kernels stir-fried. Roasting the unripe maize on the cob with the husk-on is common practice in Nepal. At our home, we love eating roasted unripe maize with buttermilk and salt-*timmur*-green chilli achaar.

Roasting
6–8 unripe maize with the husk-on
½ teaspoon *timmur*
1 teaspoon salt
2-3 green chillies

Stir-frying
4–6 unripe maize
½ teaspoon cumin seed
½ teaspoon sugar
½ teaspoon salt
1-2 tablespoons ghee

*serves 3–4 people

Roasting

Start a wood fire and make space to hold the maize over the fire. Place the maize with the husk-on over the fire and let them roast on all sides turning occasionally until almost all the husk is burnt off and the kernels start roasting. Let the maize rest for a few minutes and remove the burnt husk. If all sides aren't roasted properly, put the maize directly on the embers and roast all the sides turning it a few times.

Roasted unripe maize is best eaten with buttermilk and achaar made by grinding salt, *timmur*, and green chillies together.

Stir-frying

First remove the husk and silks or hairs of fresh unripe maize. Take off the soft milky kernels from the cobs using your hands or a knife.

Heat the ghee or butter in a pan over medium heat. Fry the cumin seeds and then add the maize kernels. Add a little salt and sugar, and stir-fry for about 10–12 minutes stirring occasionally. The kernels when cooked turn light brown. Turn off the heat and eat when still hot.

Achaar

ESSENTIAL RELISH IN NEPALI CUISINES

My mother would roast a small variety of tomatoes on firewood embers until the outer skins were burnt. She would grind freshly picked mint leaves, garlic, green chillies, and salt together on a flat stone mortar and pestle until they turn into a fine paste. This stone mortar-and-pestle, known as *silauto*, is an essential in every Nepali kitchen. She would then remove the burnt skins of the roasted tomatoes and grind them with the paste to make a spicy and tangy tomato achaar. Oftentimes, she would use other herbs and oil seeds. The piquant flavour of chilli, the acidity of the tomato, the aroma from the herb, and the nuttiness of oil seeds whet the appetite and enhance the flavour of the entire meal.

Fermented achaar is a common relish in the Nepali kitchen. Before winter, when there is an abundance of radishes in the garden, my mother ferments them to make achaar. First she would cut the radish into small fingers and let them partially dry under the sun. She would add mustard seed grounds, salt, chillies, and the spice tempering of mustard oil, turmeric powder, and fenugreek seeds. She would then fill the mixture in jars and leave for at least a couple of weeks to ferment.

The achaar-making culture traverses the southern plains to the northern highlands, across all ethnicities and communities. It is an intrinsic part of Nepali food culture and heritage, as no meal is complete without some kind of achaar. People eat it with *daal-bhat-tarkari* and roti as a side relish, and as a dipping sauce for a variety of dishes. The sharp taste of spicy, salty, and sour notes, and sometimes even a numbing sensation and sweetness, characterise achaar.

Besides freshly ground (*pineko* achaar) and fermented (*gaadeko* achaar), achaar is also made by cooking (*pakako* achaar), and by mixing fresh or boiled vegetables with spices and oil seed grounds (*moleko* achaar).

A wide variety of ingredients, from fresh vegetables, potatoes, fruits, berries, beans, chillies, citrus, oil seeds, and herbs to dried fish and meat, are used to make achaar. Coriander leaves, mint, and oil seeds with tomatoes are commonly use for *pineko* achaar, which is also known as *chutney*, a word derived from *chatani* meaning 'to lick'. Wild herbs such as *jangali dhaniya* (sawtooth coriander), *gorakhpaan/marethi* (sichuan button), and wild garlic are also used

Sesame seeds are the most common oil seeds for achaar. *Bhang* (hemp seeds) is popular in the western hilly region and *philinge* or *jhuse til* (niger seeds) in the eastern hilly region. Oil seeds are also roasted, ground together with salt and dry spices, and added with a dash of *chuk* (concentrated lemon juice) to make *chhop*, a kind of dry achaar. *Chhop* can be stored for months, which makes it a convenient relish. Many communities in the hills and plains also make a delectable achaar of *sidhra* (dried fishes).

Raw and boiled vegetables are often mixed with spices and roasted oil seeds grounds. They are often seasoned with tempering spices in hot oil, a process known as *jhanne*. *Gundrukko* achaar, which is prepared from sun-dried fermented greens, is the most beloved achaar and a signature specialty of Nepali cuisine, especially in hills.

When in season, bitter gourds, young unripe bananas, banana blossoms, *koiraloko phool* (mountain ebony flower), and *dumri* (a small fig variety) are boiled or steamed and then mixed with spices. At my paternal grandmother's home, a simple and easy green papaya achaar is usually prepared during the religious and festive gatherings, which pairs well with *selroti* and *puri*.

Vegetables, generally after being partially sun-dried, are mixed with spices, salt, and oil, and put into jars to ferment. Traditionally, clay pots are used and put into a pit to ferment. Fermentation is an important preservation technique in Nepal. Fermented pickles can last a few weeks to years.

Typically used in hilly and mountainous cuisines, *timmur* is a beloved flavouring ingredient. Mustard oil is the traditional cooking medium, which is also used to flavour achaars. Kathmandu's Newa community has a long tradition of making *buchika* (roasted

mustard oil), which is unique to Newa cuisine. Mustard seeds are roasted and then pressed in a traditional pressing machine to extract the oil, which has a smoky, aromatic, nutty, and slightly pungent flavour. A tablespoon is enough to transform the flavour of *chhyola* and achaar.

The Sherpa community uses fresh or fermented dregs of buttermilk to make achaar and flavour soups. Eastern hilly communities adore achaar of *dalle* chilli for its flavour and intense heat.

One key characteristic of achaar is its acidity, which usually comes from lemon or *chuk* or from lacto-fermentation. In Kathmandu and the surrounding areas, people use *lapsi*, which lends a peculiar sourness. They also cook and ferment whole *lapsis* to make achaar. People use the dried unripe mango as a souring and flavouring ingredient in the southern plains and the concentrated sea buckthorn in the higher Himalayan region.

The achaar variety is as varied as Nepal's ethnicity and culture. From preserving ingredients to developing new flavours, and enhancing the taste of a dish, achaar is an essential part of Nepali cuisine.

GOLBHENDAKO CHUTNEY

Roasted tomato chutney

Nepalis adore freshly ground roasted tomato chutney or achaar. Generally consumed as a relish with the main meal, it also can be used as a dipping sauce for snacks such as momo, *samosa*, *pakauda*, etc. Small local cherry tomatoes are favoured for making the chutney as they have a sharp tangy taste. But one can use any variety of tomatoes, and add lime juice if the tomatoes are not sour enough. Traditionally, tomatoes are roasted on hot charcoal in a firewood stove, and the chutney is prepared by grinding them on a mortar and pestle. One can roast tomatoes in a pan or directly over the gas flame or steam them. Even raw tomatoes can be used to make chutney.

Edible oil seeds such as sesame seeds, pumpkin seeds, hemp seeds, etc. and herbs such as coriander leaves, sawtooth coriander, mint, etc. are often used to make the tomato chutney. Oil seeds are roasted in a pan first before grinding with tomatoes. Wild aromatic spices such as *timmur*, *siltimmur*, *chimphing*, *gorakhpaan/marethi* are also used to flavour achaar. Mint, known as *pudina* or *patina*, is one of my favourite herbs for chutney. This general recipe can be used for making tomato achaar with any other herbs and oil seeds.

8–10 cherry tomatoes,
or 3 medium-sized tomatoes
A handful of mint
1–2 garlic cloves
1–3 fresh chillies
1 lemon, optional
Salt as per taste

Roast 8–10 cherry tomatoes or 4 medium-sized tomatoes on all sides over firewood charcoal until the outer skins are burnt. Or place the tomatoes in a small cast-iron pan and heat over medium heat. To peel off the skins, cover hot roasted tomatoes with a lid for a couple of minutes, which will ease the peeling. I prefer to make chutney with the burnt skin-on as it imparts a charred smoky flavour.

Add a handful of fresh mint leaves, garlic, green chillies, and salt (to taste) in a mortar and pestle, and grind them to a fine paste. Then add roasted tomatoes and grind until the mixture becomes a fine paste. Squeeze some lemon juice to give it a sharp tangy taste. The chutney is ready.

TIMMUR RA GOLBHENDAKO ACHAAR

Nepali pepper and tomato achaar

Spicy and piquant with tingling sensations, this is the most popular achaar among Nepali communities living in the foothills and mountainous regions. Easy to make, it is commonly eaten as a relish with *daal-bhat-tarkari* and also used as dipping sauce for roti, momo, and fries.

8–10 cherry tomatoes,
or 3 medium-sized tomatoes
1 teaspoon *timmur*
1–2 garlic cloves
1–3 fresh red chillies or ½ teaspoon red chilli powder
1 lemon, optional
Salt as per taste

Roast a teaspoon of *timmur* in a small pan while shaking the pan constantly until it becomes aromatic (be careful not to burn the *timmur*). It should take less than a minute over medium heat. Roast the tomatoes on all sides until the outer skins are burnt. One can use a small cast-iron pan to roast the tomatoes. Let them cool down and peel off the skins.

Grind the roasted *timmur* and salt in a mortar and pestle, or use an electric grinder. Add the garlic cloves and fresh red chillies (or dry red chilli powder), and grind them. Then add the roasted tomatoes and grind again until it becomes a fine paste. Squeeze some lemon juice if preferred.

SIDHRAKO ACHAAR

Dried small fish achaar

Sidhra (smoke-dried or sun-dried small fishes) is a delicacy in many ethnic communities. Small freshwater fish are cleaned and then smoke-dried or sun-dried for several days to preserve them. In the Tharu community, *sidhra* is a cultural food and many dishes are prepared from it. The smoke-dried fish has a slightly bitter and smoky flavour, and makes a delicious achaar, one of my favourites. It can be made into achaar on its own or with roasted tomatoes.

A small handful of *sidhra*
½ teaspoon of *timmur*, optional
3–4 roasted tomatoes
1–2 garlic cloves
1–2 fresh chillies
1 lemon, optional
Salt as per taste

Heat or roast the smoke-dried fish in a small pan. Stir or shake the pan continuously until an aroma releases, and then transfer them to a bowl to cool down. Roast the *timmur* in the same pan and transfer it to the bowl.

If you are using a mortar and pestle, grind the fish, *timmur*, and salt first. Then add the garlic and chillies, and grind them into a fine paste. Add the roasted tomatoes and grind them together. Squeeze some lemon juice if preferred. If using an electric grinder, add all the ingredients including some lemon juice and grind them together until they become a fine sauce.

GUNDRUK RA BHATMASKO ACHAAR

Dried fermented greens and roasted soybeans achaar

The peculiar tangy flavour from *gundruk* is what makes the *gundruk ra bhatmasko* achaar delectable. Most hill communities of Nepal consume this achaar often. It is commonly eaten with *daal-bhat-tarkari* or roti as a side dish. In rural regions, this achaar, served with roasted maize or roti, makes for a midday snack *(arni)* for farmers.

A handful of *gundruk*
½ cup soybeans
1 medium-sized onion, optional
3–4 garlic cloves
A half thumb-sized ginger
½ teaspoon coriander seeds
½ teaspoon cumin seeds
½ teaspoon roasted *timmur*
½ teaspoon turmeric powder
2–4 dried red chillies
2–3 green chillies, optional
A few stalks of fresh coriander leaves
2–3 tablespoons roasted mustard oil, or any regular vegetable oil
1 lemon, optional
Salt as per taste

Soak the *gundruk* in hot water for around 12–15 minutes.

Roast the soybeans in a pan until they crack and turn light brown, and transfer them to a bowl.

Make a spice paste by grinding the coriander seeds, cumin seeds, roasted *timmur*, dried red chillies, garlic, and ginger together with about a tablespoon of water in a mortar and pestle or an electric grinder.

Squeeze the soaked *gundruk* gently to drain the water. Chop them into small pieces if necessary, and smash them in a mortar and pestle to make it tender. Smashing also helps the *gundruk* absorb the spices better.

Transfer the smashed *gundruk* to a large salad bowl. Add the roasted soybeans, spice paste, salt, finely chopped onion, fresh coriander leaves, and green chillies. In a pan, heat 2–3 tablespoons of roasted mustard oil or any vegetable oil, and add the turmeric powder. Immediately turn off the heat and pour the hot oil into the achaar. Squeeze some lemon juice for more acidity, and mix all the ingredients together by hand.

KOIRALOKO PHOOLKO ACHAAR

Mountain ebony flower achaar

Koiralo (Bauhinia variegata) can be found up to an altitude of 1,900 metres. It starts flowering in the beginning of spring and the flowering lasts for only a couple of weeks. The flower has a beautiful colour, a combination of white and pink. Among the few edible flowers consumed in Nepal, *koiraloko phool* (mountain ebony flower) is the most common.

We have a *koiralo* tree, which is almost the same age as me and it gives plenty of flowers every year. I grew up eating them. When the flowers are abundant, my mother shares them with relatives and neighbours. The freshly harvested flowers are boiled in water, and then mixed with roasted sesame seed powder and spices to make an achaar. They are also steamed and then sun-dried for preservation, then later made into an achaar or curry. In Patan, its achaar is prepared by the Newa community during the Ghode Jatra or Pahachare festival feast, which falls around its flowering time. The flowers and bark are also considered to have a medicinal value, and are used to cure diarrhea and digestive problems. The Tharu community even consumes its young leaves as a vegetable.

400–500 gm *koiraloko phool* (mountain ebony flower)
3–4 medium-sized potatoes
1 medium-sized onion
2–3 green chillies
A few stalks of green garlic leaves, optional
A few stalks of fresh coriander leaves
2 tablespoons sesame seeds
1 teaspoon *timmur*
1 teaspoon coriander seeds
1 teaspoon cumin seeds
1 teaspoon fenugreek seeds
2–3 dried red chillies
1 teaspoon turmeric powder
2–3 tablespoons mustard oil, or any regular vegetable oil
1 lime/lemon
Salt as per taste

Boil or steam the *koiraloko phool* for about 10–12 minutes over medium heat or until they become tender. Remove the flowers and transfer to a large bowl immediately.

Boil the potatoes until cooked; peel the skins off once they cool down. Cut or break the potatoes with your hands into small pieces and add to the boiled flowers in the bowl.

In a pan, roast the coriander, cumin and sesame seeds, and *timmur* together until they become light brown and aromatic. Shake the pan frequently when roasting. Let them cool down and grind together in a mortar and pestle. Add the grounds over the boiled flowers and potatoes.

Chop the onion, green garlic leaves, coriander leaves, and green chillies, and add them to the bowl.

In a small pan, heat about 2–3 tablespoons of mustard oil, and fry the fenugreek seeds and dry red chillies. When the seeds start to turn brown, turn off the heat and immediately pour the hot oil over the mixture for seasoning. Squeeze some lemon juice and mix them together using your hand. The achaar is ready.

Kerako bunga (banana blossoms), young green bananas, *dumri* (cluster fig; *Ficus racemosa*), *maingatta* (emetic nut; *Xeromphis spinosa*) are also used to make achaar. Follow the same recipe to make their achaar. While using banana blossoms, remove the outer thick reddish bracts and use only the yellow-tipped florets beneath the bracts. Remove the central pistil, which is not tender or pleasant to eat. Cut young green bananas, *dumri*, and *maingatta* to bite-sized pieces after boiling them.

KARELAKO ACHAAR

Bitter gourd achaar

I love the taste of bitter gourd. Bitter gourd can be cooked as a curry, a soup with buttermilk *(kadi)*, fried, fermented, or boiled to make an achaar. Boiling or frying bitter gourd and using lemon juice helps in tempering its bitterness. The Magars, Gurungs, and other communities prepare this achaar as well.

500–600 gm bitter gourds
1 medium-sized onion
2–3 green chillies
2–3 garlic cloves
2 tablespoons sesame seeds
1 teaspoon mustard seeds
1 teaspoon *timmur* (Nepali pepper)
1 teaspoon cumin and coriander powder, optional
1 teaspoon fenugreek seeds
2–3 dried red chillies
1 teaspoon turmeric powder
2–3 tablespoons mustard oil-
or any regular vegetable oil
2 teaspoons *chuk* (concentrated lemon juice)
or 2 lemons
Salt as per taste

Cut the bitter gourds into small fingers, and boil them in water with some salt and a lemon juice or a teaspoon of *chuk* for around 12–15 minutes or until they become tender, but still retain their colour and crunchy texture. Turn off the heat, drain the water, and wash the bitter gourds with clean cold water to stop them from cooking further. Transfer them to a large bowl.

Roast the sesame seeds, mustard seeds, and *timmur* together in a pan shaking it constantly. Once the seeds start to pop, turn off the heat and transfer them to a mortar and pestle. Once they cool down, grind them to powder and add to the bitter gourds.

Finely chop the onion and chillies, and add to the bowl.

In a small pan, heat about 2–3 tablespoons of mustard oil to temper the spices. Fry the fenugreek seeds, dry red chillies, and finely chopped garlic. When the seeds start to pop and the garlic becomes light brown, add the turmeric and cumin-coriander powder. Immediately turn off the heat and pour into the bowl for seasoning.

Squeeze some lime or lemon juice or add *chuk*, and mix them together. Make sure that the spices are mixed well with the bitter gourds. The delicious achaar has a spicy, tangy, nutty, and smoky flavour, along with a slight bitterness and crunchy texture.

BADAM SANDHEKO

Spicy peanut salad

Badam sandheko is an easy snack that one can have at any time of the day. It pairs well with drinks too. Traditionally, roasted soybeans are used instead of peanuts. Both roasted soybeans and peanuts are easily available in Nepali restaurants as snacks or starters. *Badam sandheko* is easy and quick to make. The rich nutty flavour of the peanuts is balanced by a tangy and spicy flavour.

1 cup whole peanuts
1 small-size red onion
2–3 medium-sized tomatoes
2–3 fresh chillies
4–5 garlic cloves
1 thumb-sized ginger, optional
½ teaspoon red chilli powder
A few stalks fresh coriander leaves
1 lemon
1–2 tablespoons roasted mustard oil or regular vegetable oil
Salt as per taste

Roast the peanuts in a pan over medium heat for about 8–10 minutes or until they start to crack and the outer skins becomes slightly dark. Shake the pan or stir constantly while roasting. Let the peanuts cool down. Rub the peanuts with hands to break them into halves and remove the outer skins. Transfer the peanuts to a big salad bowl.

Finely slice an onion, garlic, ginger, fresh chillies, tomatoes, and coriander leaves, and add to the bowl.

Add the red chilli powder and salt (to taste). Squeeze a lemon for some acidity and drizzle 1–2 tablespoons of roasted mustard oil or any vegetable oil. Roasted mustard oil has a smoky, nutty, peppery, and lightly pungent flavour.

Mix all the ingredients well. This light and healthy snack can be eaten as an appetiser or as a snack with drinks.

PINDALU BHUJURIKO ACHAAR

Dried grated taro achaar

Taro leaves, petioles, and tubers can all be consumed by making a wide variety of dishes. Taro tubers *(pindalu)* can be steamed and cooked as a curry or soup. Tubers can also be grated and sun-dried, which is known as *pindaluko bhujuri*, and later prepared as achaar. Nowadays, this particular style is uncommon and almost forgotten. In my home, we still make it when we have an abundant harvest of taro tubers and use it all year round.

1 cup *pindalu bhujuri* (dried grated taro tuber)
2–3 tomatoes
1 small-size red onion
1–2 fresh green chillies
½ teaspoon *timmur*
½ teaspoon fenugreek seeds
½ teaspoon turmeric powder
½ teaspoon cumin powder
A few stalks of fresh coriander leaves
1 lemon
2–3 tablespoons mustard oil
  or regular vegetable oil
Salt as per taste

Soak the *pindaluko bhujuri* in hot water for about 10–15 minutes. Then drain the water and transfer the *bhujuri* to a large bowl.

Roast the *timmur* in a small pan. Grind it in a mortar and pestle, and sprinkle over the *bhujuri*. In the same pan, roast the tomatoes, let them cool, peel the skins off, add them to the bowl with the *bhujuri*, and mash them to form a paste. Finely slice the onion, fresh coriander leaves and green chillies, and add to the *bhujuri* mixture.

In a small pan, heat about 2–3 tablespoons of mustard oil or regular vegetable oil over medium heat. Fry the fenugreek seeds and add the turmeric, cumin, and red chilli powder. When the seeds start to pop, turn off the heat, and pour over the mixture for seasoning. Add salt, squeeze some lemon juice, and mix them well, preferably by hand. Garnish with the fresh coriander leaves and the achaar is ready.

GADEKO MULAKO ACHAAR

Fermented radish achaar

When radishes are in season (and abundant), they are preserved by fermentation. Fermentation gives radishes a peculiar sour flavour, and spices added to the achaar give aroma and complexity. This is the most common fermented pickle in Nepali kitchens. Other vegetables such as cauliflower, bamboo shoots, carrots, cucumber, and bitter gourds or a mix of them are also commonly used to make fermented achaar.

1 kg radishes
6–8 fresh green/red chillies
1 tablespoon red chilli powder
4–5 tablespoons mustard seeds
1 teaspoon turmeric powder
1 teaspoon fenugreek seeds
4–5 tablespoons mustard oil or regular vegetable oil
Salt as per taste

Wash the radishes and cut into one-inch-long fingers. Keep the radish fingers in direct sunlight for a day or two for partial removal of moisture. Alternatively, sprinkle about two tablespoons of salt and a teaspoon of turmeric powder, and let rest for a couple of hours, which draws water out of the radish. This way, the achaar won't become soggy. Sun-drying also adds a peculiar flavour to the achaar.

In a large bowl, add partially-dried radish fingers, green chillies cut in half, red chilli powder, and salt. Grind mustard seeds coarsely and add to the mixture.

Heat about 2–3 tablespoons of mustard oil in a small pan and fry the fenugreek seeds and turmeric powder. When the seeds start popping, turn off the heat and pour the oil over the radish and spice mixture. Mix them well using hand. Then put them into clean glass jars; press the radish fingers and tap the jars frequently to make sure they are compactly filled in.

Pour 2–3 tablespoons of mustard oil into the glass jars and put the lid on. This will check the mould formation. Put the jars in direct sunlight for at least a week to let the radish ferment. The achaar will develop flavour by that time and will be ready to be eaten. It can be allowed to ferment further. The achaar can easily be preserved for several months to a year or more.

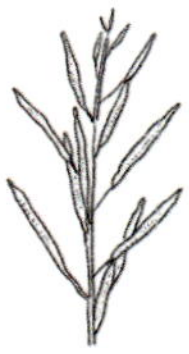

BHADAURE KANKROKO ACHAAR

Fermented Nepali cucumber achaar

Bhadaure kankroko achaar, also known as *khalpi*, is prepared during Dashain and Tihar at our home, and has become part of our festive food culture. My mother makes it a few days before the festivals every year. The achaar helps in digestion of the heavy meat-laden feasts consumed during the festivals.

Bhadaure kankro is a local variety of cucumber, named after the Nepali month of Bhadra when they are fully ripe for harvesting. The month falls just before the festive season. This variety of cucumber can weigh several kilograms and has a thick brown skin when it's fully ripe. It used to be grown abundantly in the hills, but is now slowly disappearing.

1 medium-sized *bhadaure-kankro* (Nepali cucumber)
8–10 *dalle khursani* (Himalayan round chillies) or regular fresh green/red chillies
4–5 tablespoons mustard seeds
1 tablespoon red chilli powder
1 tablespoon turmeric powder
1 teaspoon fenugreek seeds
½ cup of mustard oil, or regular vegetable oil

Wash the cucumber with clean water and cut into quarters as elongated slices. Remove the soft pulp, including the seeds with a knife. Do not throw away the pulp; it can be made into a salad/achaar. If the girth of the cucumber is large, slice each quarter into halves. Then cut the cucumber into inch-long chunks. Make a couple of incisions on the flesh as this will help the cucumber chunks dry quickly and absorb the spices as well.

Keep the chunks in sunlight for a day or two to remove some moisture. This prevents the achaar from becoming watery and also helps retain a nice crunchy texture. Sun-drying imparts a peculiar flavour to the achaar. Alternatively, sprinkling about 2–3 tablespoons of salt and putting aside for a couple of hours will draw out some moisture.

In a large bowl, mix the partially sun-dried cucumber pieces, chillies cut in half, coarsely ground mustard seeds, red chilli powder, and salt.

In a small pan, heat around 2–3 tablespoons of mustard
oil or regular vegetable oil, fry the fenugreek seeds, and then add the turmeric powder. Turn off the heat and immediately pour the hot oil over the cucumber. Mix thoroughly using your hand.

Compact the mixture into a clean glass jar. Then pour 2–3 tablespoons of vegetable oil in the jar. Keep the jars in direct sunlight for 2–3 days to let the cucumber ferment. It is generally best to eat the achaar within a week, as it will lose its crunchiness after a while. The pickle has a peculiar sourness from the fermentation, a crunchy yet soft texture, and heat from the chillies and the mustard seeds.

To make a salad from the cucumber pulp, first remove the seeds, and add some finely chopped onions, fresh green/red chillies, and fresh coriander leaves to the pulp in a bowl. Then add a pinch of turmeric powder, cumin powder, timmur grounds, and salt. Mix them together. This makes an easy and refreshing salad.

GOLBHENDA RA MULAKO BIUKO ACHAAR

Raw tomato and radish seed achaar

This achaar, made from raw tomatoes, radish seeds and spices, is simply delicious. A hint of peppery taste comes from the radish seeds, and fermentation develops a peculiar tangy flavour. As far as I know, the Newas are the only ethnic group that uses radish seeds as a flavouring ingredient. A Newa friend introduced me to this pickle and provided me with the recipe. The longer you ferment the pickle, the tangier it becomes.

1 kg tomatoes
3–4 tablespoons radish seeds
1 tablespoon mustard seeds, optional
6–8 garlic cloves
1 large thumb-sized ginger
6–8 green chillies
1 teaspoon fenugreek seeds
1 teaspoon turmeric powder
1 tablespoon red chilli powder
7–8 tablespoons vegetable oil, preferably mustard oil
Salt as per taste

Clean the tomatoes, chop them into small pieces, and transfer to a large bowl. Press the tomatoes very gently and remove excess water. Finely chop the green chillies, ginger, and garlic cloves, and add to the bowl.

Lightly roast the radish seeds and mustard seeds (optional) in a pan, stirring constantly. As soon as they start to pop, turn off the heat and transfer them to a mortar and pestle. Allow them to cool and grind coarsely. Add the coarsely ground radish and mustard seeds, as well as the turmeric powder, red chilli powder, and salt to the tomatoes.

In a small pan, heat 5–6 tablespoons of mustard oil and fry the fenugreek seeds. Turn off the heat when the seeds start to turn brown, and immediately pour the oil over the tomatoes and spices. Mix them properly.

Transfer the mixture to a clean glass jar. Tap or lightly shake the jar occasionally while filling. This will help prevent air pockets. Fill the jar just below the neck as it boils up during fermentation. Heat two tablespoons of mustard oil, pour it into the jar, and close the lid tightly. This will help prevent mould formation at the surface of the jar.

Leave for about a week in sunlight, which facilitates fermentation and prevents mould. In that duration, the pickle will develop a sour flavour and will be ready to eat. The radish and mustard seeds give a peppery, pungent and nutty flavour to the achaar. It can be preserved for several months.

DALLE KHURSANIKO ACHAAR

Himalayan round chilli achaar

Dalle or *akbare khursani* (Himalayan round chilli) is one of the hottest chillies in the world. There is another local variety of extremely hot chilli called *jire khursani*, a tiny chilli that is apparently the size of a cumin seed, from which it derives its name. This chilli variety is very rare to find now. *Dalle khursani* is round in shape and bright red when fully ripe. The chilli also has sweet, fruity notes.

Dalle khursani is grown and widely consumed, especially in the mid-hills of eastern Nepal. People prefer to eat the chilli during the cold winter months as the heat warms the body. Although the chilli is hot, it surprisingly doesn't leave any burning sensations in the stomach like other chillies. It is also believed to have medicinal benefits. The chilli can simply be pickled with just vinegar and salt, a very common recipe.

½ kg *dalle/akbare khursani*
2–3 tablespoons ginger paste
2–3 tablespoons garlic paste
2–3 tablespoons yellow mustard seeds
1 teaspoon coriander powder
1 teaspoon cumin powder
1 teaspoon turmeric powder
1 teaspoon red chilli powder
1 teaspoon fenugreek seeds
½ cup vegetable oil, preferably mustard oil
1 lemon/lime
Salt as per taste

In a pan, heat around half a cup of vegetable oil, preferably mustard oil. Fry the fenugreek seeds, and then the garlic and ginger paste. Fry until they turn light brown. Turn off the heat and add the turmeric powder, red chilli powder, coarsely ground mustard seeds, salt, and some lemon juice. Let the spice mixture cool.

Add whole *dalle khursani* to the pan with the spice mixture, and mix thoroughly. Transfer the mixture to a clean and dry glass jar. Pour a few tablespoons of mustard or vegetable oil into the jar. Close the jar tightly, and leave it outside in direct sunlight for at least 4–5 days. This will prevent mould formation in the pickle and facilitates fermentation. The spicy *dalle khursaniko* achaar is ready and can be stored for several months.

TAMAKO ACHAAR

Bamboo shoot achaar

Growing up, we had a small patch of bamboo trees that used to produce plenty of bamboo shoots during monsoon. Some young shoots were harvested for consumption while others were left to grow. In season, these shoots are widely consumed in Nepal. Fresh shoots are simply cooked as a curry. When in abundance, they are preserved by fermentation. One way of preserving them is to put slices of bamboo shoots in a jar, which is later consumed as a curry or soup. Another fermentation method is to mix the shoots with spices and salt to make achaar. The fermented bamboo shoots have a peculiar acidic flavour. The recipe for the achaar is similar to fermented radish achaar.

1 kg bamboo shoots
6–8 fresh green/red chillies
1 tablespoon red chilli powder
3–4 tablespoons mustard seeds
1 teaspoon turmeric powder
1 teaspoon fenugreek seeds
4–5 tablespoons mustard or any vegetable oil
Salt as per taste

Remove the tough outer layers or skins of the bamboo shoots until you find the tender and compact flesh. Halve or quarter the bamboo shoots, depending on the size, and cut into thin slices. Wash the slices and immerse them in water for a couple of hours (preferably overnight) in a large pot. This reduces the bitterness.

Remove the slices and transfer them to a large bowl. Lightly roast the mustard seeds, grind them coarsely, and add to the bowl. Add the red chilli powder, halved chillies, and salt.

Heat about 2–3 tablespoons of mustard oil in a small pan, fry the fenugreek seeds, and then add the turmeric powder. Pour the oil immediately over the bamboo shoots and spices mixture. Mix them well using your hand. Then compact them into clean and dry glass jars. Pour 1–2 tablespoons of mustard oil again into the glass jars and put the lid on. This will help check the formation of mould. For fermentation, put the jars in direct sunlight for at least a week. The achaar will be ready to eat by that time and can be stored for several months to a year.

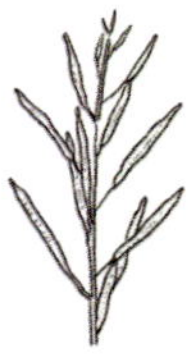

SUKUTIKO ACHAAR

Smoke-dried meat achaar

During festivals, when meat is abundant, it is smoke-dried for preservation. Every year, after Dashain and Tihar, we make achaar from smoke-dried buffalo meat. Smoke-dried meat (*sukuti*) is made using lean meat that is cut into thick strips and hung over a firewood stove for a few hours to smoke. They are placed at a considerable height from the fire to slowly dry the meat. The *sukuti* is then furthur sun-dried for a day or two.

200–250 gm buffalo *sukuti*
5-6 tablespoons ginger paste
2–3 tablespoons garlic paste
6–8 fresh green/red chillies
1–2 tablespoons red chilli powder
½ tablespoon turmeric powder
1 tablespoon cumin and coriander powder mix
½ cup mustard oil
1 lemon
Salt as per taste

Cut the *sukuti* into small pieces. If it is too dry or tough to cut, smash it lighlty with a pestle and soak in hot water for about half an hour to make it softer.

Heat about half a cup of mustard oil in a pan over medium heat. Add the *sukuti* pieces and fry for a few minutes. Then add the ginger and garlic paste, and cook until light brown. Add the chopped fresh chillies, salt, and turmeric, cumin, coriander, and red chilli powder. Squeeze lemon juice and cook further for a couple of minutes while stirring occasionally. Turn off the heat and transfer all the mixture to a clean and dry glass jar. Close the jar, and set aside for a week so that the *sukuti* will soak up all the spices and become more flavourful.

GOLBHENDA, TIL RA MULAKO BIUKO ACHAAR

Tomato achaar with sesame and radish seeds

The slightly nutty, pungent, and bitter flavour from radish seeds is what makes this achaar delicious. This recipe is from the mother of a Newa friend.

1 kg tomatoes
5–6 garlic cloves
1 thumb-sized ginger
4 tablespoons sesame seeds
4 tablespoons radish seeds
1 teaspoon *timmur*
8–10 fresh red/green chillies
1 tablespoon red chilli powder
1 teaspoon turmeric powder
1 tablespoon *jimbu*
1 teaspoon fenugreek seeds
5–6 tablespoons vegetable oil
1 lemon, preferably *jhamsi* (local citrus fruit)
Salt as per taste

In a small pan, lightly roast the sesame seeds, radish seeds, and *timmur* separately over medium heat. Stir continuously in order to roast the seeds evenly; make sure to put the lid on once the seeds start popping. Transfer to a plate to cool them down and grind coarsely in a mortar and pestle or an electric grinder.

Cut tomatoes and grind them into a paste using a blender or a large mortar and pestle.

To make achaar, heat about two tablespoons of vegetable oil in a pan over medium heat. When the oil is hot, fry the fenugreek seeds and *jimbu*. Then add the tomato paste into the pan. Add the turmeric powder, red chilli powder and salt, and cook for about 10–12 minutes over low heat with an occasional stir.

While the tomato paste is cooking, smash the garlic cloves and ginger, and mince them. Also, chop the green chillies. Heat 4–5 tablespoons of oil in another small pan. Add the minced garlic and ginger, and fry for a few minutes or until light brown. Add the chopped green chillies and cook for another minute. Add the sesame and radish seed grounds, a pinch of salt, and turmeric powder. Stir the mixture, turn off the heat, and add the mixture to the cooking tomatoes.

Squeeze a *jhamsi*, or alternatively lemon, and add a teaspoon of roasted timmur grounds. Cook the tomato mixture for another 20 minutes over low heat, stirring occasionally until it becomes thick and the oil starts to surface. The cooked tomato achaar is ready; transfer to clean, dry jars, pour 1–2 tablespoons of hot vegetable oil into the jars for preservation and close them. The achaar can be stored for a couple of weeks without refrigeration.

GOLBHENDA, MULA RA SANO KERAUKO ACHAAR

Tomato, radish, and field pea achaar

This is a common achaar prepared by cooking radish, peas, and tomatoes together. The process is similar to that of making curry. Easy to make, this achaar is mainly prepared during festivals and large gatherings.

1 kg tomatoes
1 medium-sized radish
½ cup dried field peas *(sano kerau)* or fresh peas *(hariyo kerau)*
1 medium-sized onion
5–6 garlic cloves
1 thumb-sized ginger
5–6 fresh green/red chillies
1 tablespoon cumin and coriander powder mix
1 teaspoon red chilli powder
1 teaspoon turmeric powder
1 teaspoon fenugreek seeds
1 lemon
3–4 tablespoons vegetable oil, preferably mustard oil
Fresh coriander leaves, for garnishing
Salt as per taste

If you are using dried field peas, soak them in water for several hours or overnight. When the peas are fully soaked, wash them and drain.

Dice the tomatoes and cut the radish into small fingers. Grind the ginger and garlic into a paste in a mortar and pestle. Finely slice the onion and chillies.

In a pan, heat 3–4 tablespoons of vegetable oil (preferably mustard oil) over medium heat. Fry the fenugreek seeds and then the sliced onion. When the onions become soft, add the ginger and garlic paste and fry until light brown. Then add the turmeric powder, fresh green/red chillies, and tomatoes. When the tomatoes start to melt, add the cumin-coriander powder, red chilli powder, and salt. Give it a stir and cook for a couple of minutes. Then add the radish and peas, and cook them for another 15 minutes or so, stirring occasionally. Squeeze some lemon juice and also add some water in between if necessary. Turn off the heat and garnish the achaar with the fresh coriander leaves. Eat as a side dish with rice or roti.

GULIYO LAPSIKO ACHAAR

Sweet lapsi achaar

Known locally as *lapsi* (Nepali hog plum), a local sour fruit native to Nepal, it is a popular fruit for making achaar and as a souring agent in the Kathmandu Valley and surrounding regions. It has a peculiar sour taste and aroma, with a hint of sweetness. An important ingredient in Newa food culture, it is used to make a sour soup *paunkwa*, an essential in every feast. It is also used to make sweets and fruit leathers. Dried *lapsi* skin powder is also widely used as a souring ingredient in achaar. The sweet and spicy version of the achaar is most common in the Nepali kitchen.

1 kg *lapsi*
1 ½ cups sugar
2-3 bay leaves
3-4 dried red chillies
1 teaspoon cinnamon powder
½ teaspoon turmeric powder
1 teaspoon fenugreek seeds
1 teaspoon cumin seeds
7–8 tablespoons vegetable oil
Salt as per taste

Boil the *lapsi* in a pot with about a cup of water for around 20 minutes or until the outer skin breaks. If using a pressure cooker, cook for two whistles. Let the *lapsi* cool down and peel the skin using your hand. The skin can be sun-dried for later use as a souring agent.

In a cooking pan, heat 5–6 tablespoons of vegetable oil. When the oil is hot enough, add the fenugreek seeds, cumin seeds, bay leaves, and dried red chillies. When the seeds start popping, add the turmeric powder and immediately add the peeled *lapsis*. Stir and add about one and half cups of sugar, some salt, cinnamon and red chilli powder, and a few tablespoons of water. Cook for about 20–25 minutes over low-medium heat, stirring occasionally. Sugar caramelises to a light brown colour. Add more sugar if you prefer to make the achaar sweeter.

Turn off the heat, let it cool a little, and transfer it to clean dry glass jars. Tap occasionally to avoid forming air pockets. Pour 1–2 tablespoons of vegetable oil and close the lids. The achaar will last for several months.

List of Recipes

THARU & MAITHIL CUISINES

SHERPA, TAMANG & TIBETAN CUISINES

MAGAR & GURUNG CUISINES

KHAS CUISINE

AUTHOR'S FLAVOURS

ACHAAR

Prashanta Khanal explores and writes about Nepali food culture, its history, and recipes. Having grown up in a family with different cultural backgrounds, he is interested in experiencing new flavours and understanding new food traditions and cultural diversity. He believes that food is the epitome of culture and cooking is a fundamental expression of love.

Besides indulging his palate, he works in environmental sustainability, specifically on sustainable cities, air pollution, and climate change, and also writes on the issues.

You can dip into his food related stories and recipes at ***www.thegundruk.com.***